NOVELTY

LISA TILLEY

MEREHURST

For Mum, Dad, Mel and Carrie with all my love and heartfelt thanks, always.

Published in 1995 by Merehurst Limited, Ferry House, 51 – 57 Lacy Road, Putney, London SW15 1PR

Copyright © Merehurst Limited 1995

ISBN 185391-490-8

Managing Editor Bridget Jones
Edited by Donna Wood
Designed by Jo Tapper
Photography by James Duncan
Colour separation by Global Colour, Malaysia
Printed by Wing King Tong, Hong Kong

A sincere thank you to Tony Lowe, for all his invaluable help, support, encouragement and patience, and to Gill Cartwright for his kindness and generosity in my time of need.

Acknowledgements
The author and publisher would like to thank the following for their assistance:
Anniversary House (Cake Decorations) Ltd., Unit 16, Elliott Road, West Howe Industrial Estate, Bournemouth, BH11 8LZ;
Cake Art Ltd., Venture Way, Crown Estate, Priorswood, Taunton, TA2 8DE;
Guy, Paul & Co. Ltd., Unit B4, Foundary Way, Little End Road, Eaton Socon, Cambridge PE19 3JH;
Manson Products, Warwick Road, Tyseley, Birmingham;
Squires Kitchen, Squires House, 3 Waverley Lane, Farnham, Surrey, GU9 8BB.

NOTES ON USING THE RECIPES

For all recipes, quantities are given in metric, Imperial and cup measurements. Follow one set of measures only as they are not interchangeable. Standard 5ml teaspoons (tsp) and 15ml tablespoons (tbsp) are used. Australian readers, whose tablespoons measure 20ml, should adjust quantities accordingly. All spoon measures are assumed to be level unless otherwise stated.
Eggs are a standard size 3 (medium) unless otherwise stated.

CONTENTS

INTRODUCTION

The one essential ingredient required for making a novelty cake is a sense of humour, because if you derive pleasure from making a cake, it will show through in the end result. I always say that it is the little things that matter. Simple finishing touches like trimming the edge of the board with colour co-ordinated ribbon when the cake is complete, make all the difference – as does making each cake you decorate personal in some way. The novelty cakes which make the greatest impression on the recipients are those on which there is attention to detail. It is so satisfying when someone notices what might be a tiny addition which you have included to make that cake special to them.

I like to use a good, home-made, fairly close-textured sponge as the base for novelty cakes – it is ideal for carving and shaping and it tastes good too. There is no need for expensive, fancy shaped tins; all of my novelty cakes begin as square, round, oblong or basin shapes and are then sculpted or carved as necessary. I never use any artificial decorations when producing a novelty cake – my cakes are allergic to plastic! Remember that you are always going to be hyper-critical of your own work, purely because you have been scrutinizing every last crumb in the making of your masterpiece. Believe me, no-one else will notice those little errors.

What aspiring novelty cake decorators need are ideas. I would like to think that this book will provide a few of those ideas on which you, the reader, can expand. Do not be afraid to 'have a go'. Once the work is set out in clear stages, creating an exciting novelty cake becomes less daunting – so be brave and start with one of the simpler cakes to boost your confidence before making a more detailed design. Let's face it, should you have a complete disaster you can always eat the evidence!

BASIC RECIPES AND EQUIPMENT

SPONGE CAKE

❖

This recipe makes a close-textured sponge cake which is ideal for carving and shaping.

TIN (PAN) SIZE

	15cm (6 in) square	20cm (8 in) square	20cm (8 in) round	25cm(10 in) square
Margarine	185g (6 oz/¾ cup)	315g (10 oz/1¼ cups)	250g (8 oz/1 cup)	440g (14 oz/1¾ cups)
Caster (superfine) sugar	185g (6 oz/¾ cup)	315g (10 oz/1¼ cups)	250g (8 oz/1 cup)	440g (14 oz/1¾ cups)
Eggs	3	5	4	7
Self-raising flour	185g (6 oz/¾ cup)	315g (10 oz/1¼ cups)	250g (8 oz/1 cup)	440g (14 oz/1¾ cups)
Oven temperature	180°C (350°F/Gas 4)	180°C (350°F/Gas 4)	180°C (350°F/Gas 4)	180°C (350°F/Gas 4)
Cooking time	40 minutes	1 hour 10 minutes	1 hour	1½ hours

TIN (PAN) OR CONTAINER SIZE

	15cm (6 in) basin	13cm (5 in) basin	28 x 18cm (11 x 7 in) oblong
Margarine	185g (6 oz/¾ cup)	125g (4 oz/½ cup)	315g (10 oz/1¼ cups)
Caster (superfine) sugar	185g (6 oz/¾ cup)	125g (4 oz/½ cup)	315g (10 oz/1¼ cups)
Eggs	3	2	5
Self-raising flour	185g (6 oz/¾ cup)	125g (4 oz/½ cup)	315g (10 oz/1¼ cups)
Oven temperature	180°C (350°F/Gas 4)	180°C (350°F/Gas 4)	180°C (350°F/Gas 4)
Cooking time	45 minutes	30 minutes	1 hour 10 minutes

VARIATIONS

Lemon Sponge Cake Follow the basic recipe adding the finely grated rind of 1 lemon and the juice of ½ lemon for every 185g (6 oz/¾ cup) caster (superfine) sugar. Mix the rind with the creamed margarine and sugar; fold the lemon juice into the mixture after the flour has been incorporated.

Chocolate Sponge Cake Follow the basic recipe substituting 125g (4 oz/½ cup) cocoa (unsweetened cocoa powder) for 125g (4 oz/½ cup) self-raising flour.

NOTE For the 15cm (6 in) square cake tin and the 13cm (5 in) basin, substitute 60g (2 oz/¼ cup) cocoa (unsweetened cocoa powder) for 60g (2 oz/¼ cup) self-raising flour.

Coffee Sponge Cake Follow the basic recipe adding 2 tsp coffee essence (strong black coffee) for every 90g (3 oz) of caster (superfine) sugar.

DEEP SPONGE CAKE

❖

If you require a slightly deeper sponge, add an extra 60g (2 oz/¼ cup) self-raising flour and 1 extra egg to the standard ingredients for the basin or cake tin (pan) size you are using.

● Preheat the oven to 180°C (350°F/Gas 4). Line and grease the tin (pan) with greaseproof paper (parchment). Grease a basin, then lay a strip of greaseproof paper (parchment) in it, overlapping the rim on opposite sides of the basin; grease the strip of paper. The strip of paper helps when removing the cake from the basin.

● Cream the margarine and caster (superfine) sugar together until pale and fluffy in appearance.

● Sift half the self-raising flour and add it to the creamed mixture with the eggs. Beat thoroughly until all ingredients are combined well.

● Sift the remaining flour and fold it in gently using a large metal spoon.

● Spoon the mixture into the prepared tin, making a slight well in the centre before baking to ensure that the cake does not rise too much. This will produce a flatter end result which is easier to use for novelty cakes.

● Because individual ovens vary in temperature, always check the cake 10 – 15 minutes before it is due to be cooked. It should be well risen, golden brown and spring back up when the top is lightly pressed.

EXPERT ADVICE

≈

Where possible use an electric food mixer for cake making. It is much easier to incorporate air and is generally far quicker than the old wooden spoon.

BUTTERCREAM

❖

13cm (5 in) BASIN
125g (4 oz/½ cup) butter, softened
250g (8 oz/1 cup) icing (confectioners') sugar
2 drops of vanilla essence (extract)

20CM (8 in) ROUND OR SQUARE CAKE TIN
250g (8 oz/1 cup) butter, softened
500g (1 lb/2 cups) icing (confectioners') sugar
3 drops of vanilla essence (extract)

25cm (10 in) SQUARE OR 28 x 18cm (11 x 7 in) OBLONG CAKE TIN
375g (12 oz/1½ cups) butter, softened
750g (1½ lb/3 cups) icing (confectioners') sugar
4 drops of vanilla essence (extract)

● Place the softened butter in a mixing bowl and beat until smooth. Gradually add the sifted icing (confectioners') sugar, beating after each addition until well combined.

● Add the vanilla essence (extract). The vanilla may be replaced by cocoa (unsweetened cocoa powder) or coffee.

VARIATIONS

Chocolate Buttercream Follow the basic recipe, omitting the vanilla essence (extract). Add 100g (3½ oz/½ cup) cocoa (unsweetened cocoa powder) for every 250g (8 oz/1 cup) icing (confectioners') sugar.

Coffee Buttercream Follow the basic recipe, omitting the vanilla essence (extract) and adding 2 tsp coffee essence (strong black coffee) for every 125g (4 oz/½ cup) icing (confectioners') sugar.

APRICOT GLAZE

❖

500g (1 lb/2 cups) apricot jam (conserve)
125ml (4 fl oz/½ cup) water

● Heat the apricot jam (conserve) and water together in a saucepan, stirring occasionally, until the jam melts and the mixture boils.
● Remove the mixture from the source of heat and press it through a sieve, breaking down lumps and discarding any fruit skins. The apricot glaze should be of an easy-to-spread consistency, not too runny. If it is watery, simply add more boiled and sieved apricot jam (conserve) to thicken. Use while still hot.

ROYAL ICING

❖

15g (½ oz) powdered egg white
90ml (3 fl oz) cold water
500g (1 lb) icing (confectioners') sugar
OR
3 egg whites
500g (1 lb) icing (confectioners') sugar

● Place the powdered egg white and cold water in the clean, grease-free bowl of an electric food mixer and mix thoroughly using the whisk attachment. When very slightly frothy change to the beater attachment.
● Gradually add the sifted icing (confectioners') sugar, beating until the icing is smooth and shiny. It should be the consistency of softened butter. A little more water, or alternatively icing (confectioners') sugar may be added to adjust the consistency, if required.
● When using fresh egg whites simply place them in a clean, grease-free bowl, add sifted icing (confectioners') sugar and beat until you have a smooth, shiny royal icing the consistency of softened butter.

EQUIPMENT

❖

You will not need a vast array of specialist equipment to make the cakes in this book. Everyday kitchen equipment is used in most cases with a few specialist items listed below for the decoration. Crockery and simple household items can often be used as cutters when making novelty shapes but remember to thoroughly wash and dry any items which are not normally used as kitchen equipment before using them with food.

Turntable
Acrylic rolling pins – 23cm (9 in) and 40cm (16 in) long
Plastic smoother
Paintbrushes – nos. 1,2,3,4,5,6
Palette knives – 8cm (3¼ in) blade, 10.5cm (4¼ in) blade and 15.5cm (6¼ in) blade
Cocktail sticks (toothpicks)
Knife with a sharp, tapered blade
Piping tubes (tips) – nos. 1,2,3,4,43,57
Ball modelling tool

ESSENTIAL TECHNIQUES

MAKING A PAPER PIPING BAG

Take a sheet of greaseproof paper (parchment), see 1. Fold it in half widthways and slit it in two using a knife, see 2. Fold one corner over to the opposite corner, see 3, and again cut down the fold, so that you have two triangles each with a corner cut off, see 4. Take one triangle and roll the cut corner to the middle, curling it over to form a cone, see 5. Fold the pointed end over the top and around the back of the cone, shuffling the paper until you have a good tight point at the end of the bag, see 6. Finally, make two small folds at the top of the bag to secure it and snip the point off to insert a piping tube (tip).

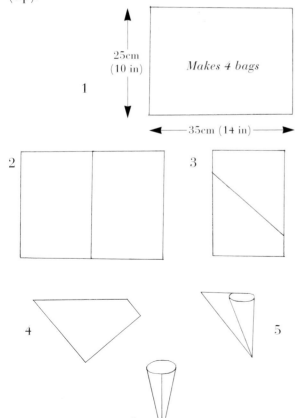

ROUNDING OFF CAKE EDGES

When a sponge cake has been cut to shape for a specific design the edges will sometimes need softening in shape to enhance the effect. This is achieved by trimming off any square edges with a sharp knife to give a more rounded appearance. This also makes the cake easier to cover with sugarpaste as the softer the edges, the less likely it is that the sugarpaste will tear.

EXPERT ADVICE

≈

I always use ready prepared sugarpaste and modelling paste which is easily obtained from any good cake-decorating supplier. Some pastes are sweeter than others so make sure that you choose the one to suit your taste.

COVERING CAKES WITH SUGARPASTE

Knead the sugarpaste thoroughly before rolling out or modelling; the warmth of your hands will make the paste more malleable and therefore easier to use.

When rolling out or modelling use a little cornflour (cornstarch) or icing (confectioners') sugar to prevent sticking; but not too much which will cause the paste to crack and dry out. If the paste does look and feel slightly dry, sprinkle a little water onto it and knead it in well. When covering a sponge cake, unless otherwise stated, roll out the paste to a depth of approximately 5mm (¼ in).

Before covering the cake always fill any holes or imperfections with sugarpaste or marzipan (almond paste) if using. This will give the coating a smooth finish. Coat the sponge cake with a layer of apricot glaze before applying sugarpaste. For an even smoother finish you may cover the cake with marzipan (almond paste) before coating with sugarpaste.

If you require a completely flat cake surface for the design you have in mind, a spirit level is very useful. However, make sure that your work surface and turntable are level before checking the cake with the level, otherwise you may start carving off pieces of cake to level it out when it is actually the work surface that is uneven! I keep a lightweight plastic spirit level for use only on my cakes.

PAINTING ONTO SUGARPASTE

Always let the sugarpaste dry out thoroughly before attempting to paint onto it. If the sugarpaste is still wet the colours will 'bleed'

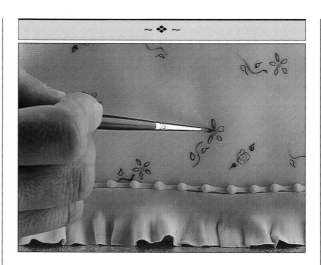

into the icing and any pattern will blur, causing a loss of definition. I use paste, liquid and powder (petal dust/blossom tint) colours for painting. Put a little of whichever colouring you choose onto a white saucer, then gradually mix in a little water to achieve the right brushing consistency. Dusting powder (petal dust/ blossom tint) may be used wet or dry.

Use a fine paintbrush for delicate patterns; if the paintbrush is too thick the pattern will look clumsy. Be careful not to lean on the cake while painting because even though the sugarpaste appears to be fairly firm, it will dent very easily. If you need support to steady your hand, lay a thin piece of card or cake board on the surface of the cake on which you can lightly rest.

Do not panic if the icing appears to be sweating – this is usually caused by humid weather or the cake being stored in a damp place. Move the cake to a dry area where air can circulate and the icing will dry out nicely.

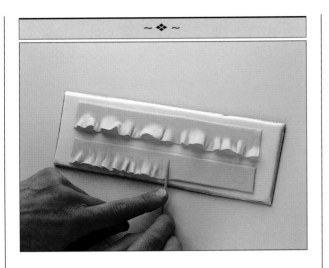

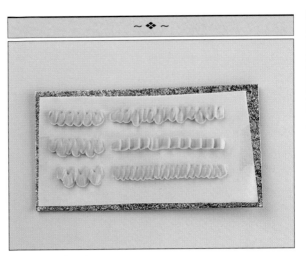

FRILLING

You will need a modelling paste for frilling. Modelling paste or gum paste is sugarpaste containing gum tragacanth. It is a drier, less sticky paste to work with than sugarpaste, which enables it to be rolled out very thinly, and it is also much harder when dry.

To make a frill, roll out the modelling paste to approximately 1mm thick. The more you work with modelling paste the more your confidence will grow, so that eventually you will be able to roll it out as thin as a sheet of paper. The thinner the paste, the finer and more delicate the finish.

Cut the paste into strips of the required width, usually 1cm (½ in). wide and to a manageable length, approximately 15 – 20cm (6 – 8 in) long. Lay the strip of paste flat on the work surface then roll a cocktail stick (toothpick) along the edge facing you, applying a little pressure until it begins to frill out.

Using a paintbrush, dampen the straight top edge facing you with a little water. Turn the strip over and apply it to the cake, attaching it with light finger pressure along the dampened edge before teasing out the bottom of the frill with a paintbrush to give a fuller effect.

PIPED FRILLING

Use a no. 57 petal piping tube (tip) to pipe a frill. Fit the tube in a piping bag and fill with royal icing. To achieve the frilled effect, shake the tube (tip) gently from side to side as you pipe. This produces gathered strips of icing which may be scalloped or straight as shown above.

MODELLING SUGARPASTE BEARS

Colour the sugarpaste dark brown. Take a piece the size of a small plum and roll it into a ball before shaping it, as shown in the photograph on page 12, for the body. Take a piece of sugarpaste half the size of the body and roll into a ball ready to model a head for the bear. Pull the sugarpaste forward with your fingers to form a muzzle. Then brush the head with a little water and attach it to the body.

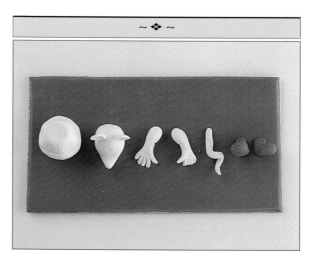

When modelling the limbs for the bears, always begin with equal-sized balls of sugarpaste for both arms and both legs, so that the end result is a well-balanced bear! Model the limbs, as shown above, tapering their ends. The legs should be turned up slightly at one end to represent feet, and the arms tapered, then shaped to form a basic hand. Brush with a little water and attach to the body.

Make round holes for eyes with the end of a paintbrush. Pipe in the whites of the eyes and a nose with a little white royal icing, using a no. 1 piping tube (tip). When dry, pipe in the blacks of the eyes and paint the nose pink.

EXPERT ADVICE

≈

When modelling with sugarpaste or modelling paste, always use a little cornflour (cornstarch) or icing (confectioners') sugar to prevent sticking. Do not use too much, or you will find that the paste will begin to dry out and crack.

MODELLING SUGARPASTE MICE

❖

Begin with a piece of paste the size of a golf or squash ball for each mouse. Use half for the body and the other half for the head, arms and legs. Using the shapes shown as a guide, model the body first, marking the crossed lines on the front and bending the paste slightly into a sitting position. Make indentations in position for the head and arms. Roll a ball of paste for the head and gradually model the long nose, curving it up slightly. Make the ears, indenting them slightly with a ball modelling tool, and carefully attach them to the top of the head by dampening the paste. Model the arms, bending them slightly at the elbows, and shape the fingers. The arms can be modelled into different positions, as shown in the photograph of the finished cake on page 35. Roll a thin tail for each mouse and curl the end. Make a pair of wellington boots for each mouse. Assemble the pieces, carefully sticking them in place with a little water. Use a cocktail stick to mark a tread pattern on the bottom of the wellington boots, then paint lightly with grey food colouring to accentuate the pattern. Leave to dry. Paint on the eyes and mouth when the paste is dry. Dust the cheeks and inside the ears with a little pink dusting powder (petal dust/blossom tint).

MODELLING SUGARPASTE FIGURES

❖

Colour the sugarpaste as required before beginning to model the figures. Roll out a piece of sugarpaste to approximately 1cm (½ in) in depth and cut out a pair of legs (trousers), approximately 4cm (1½ in) long and 2cm (¾ in) wide, as shown right. Taper the legs slightly at the top and make a cut up the centre leaving 1cm (½ in) clear at the tapered end. Soften the square edges of the trousers with your fingers.

Use a smaller piece of sugarpaste to make the body. First roll the paste into a ball, then work it with your fingers until it forms an oblong with rounded edges. Taper the oblong slightly at one end. Cut a small semi-circle from the tapered end of the body to represent the neckline and trim off the two top corners, as shown in the step-by-step photograph. Attach the body to the legs using a little royal icing. For standing figures, place a cocktail stick (toothpick) through each leg and up into the body for extra stability. Make sure that the recipient of the cake knows that there is a cocktail stick (toothpick) in the model, for safety's sake!

Model the arms out of two small pieces of sugarpaste, rolled and tapered at one end. Attach to the body using a paintbrush and a little water, then make a hole in the tapered end for a hand to be inserted. The hands are small flattened circles of flesh-coloured sugarpaste,

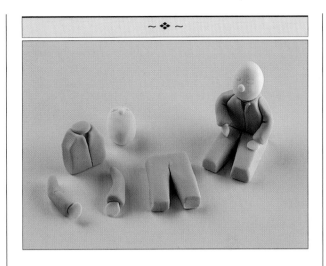

~ ❖ ~

pinched at one side to fit into the ends of the arms.

Make an oval-shaped head out of a piece of flesh-coloured sugarpaste, making almond-shaped indentations with a cocktail stick (toothpick) for the eyes. Fill the sockets with royal icing, attach a button-shaped nose and leave to dry.

Paint on facial features, including rosy cheeks, eyelashes, freckles and eyebrows. Pipe on the hair in the colour of your choice (or to match the recipient's); add glasses or other details to give the figure a personality.

AUNTIE'S FIREPLACE

25cm (10 in) square Sponge Cake, see page 6
strawberry jam (conserve), lemon curd or
Buttercream, see page 7
125ml (4 fl oz/½ cup) Royal Icing, see page 8
185ml (6 fl oz/¾ cup) Apricot Glaze,
see page 8
1.5kg (3 lb) sugarpaste
liquorice black, berry blue, melon yellow,
Christmas red, mint green, grape violet and
tangerine paste food colours
raspberry pink liquid food colouring
silver lustre powder
EQUIPMENT
30cm (12 in) square cake board
no. 1 and 2 paintbrushes
plastic smoother
no. 3 piping tube (tip)
waxed paper
ball modelling tool
cocktail stick (toothpick)
1.25m (4 ft) of 1cm (½ in) wide ribbon

● Cut off a third of the sponge cake and set it aside. Stand the remaining piece of cake up on end, longest side to the board, and cut a 5cm (2 in) strip from one end. The diagram on page 70 shows cutting lines for the cake. Trim the reserved third of sponge and place it behind the upright piece on the board to stabilize it.

● Build up both sides of the fireplace using the 5 x 18cm (2 x 7 in) strip of sponge cake, as shown in step 1.

● Sandwich all the pieces of cake together with jam (conserve) or buttercream; attach to the board with a little royal icing, then coat with apricot glaze.

● Take 1kg (2 lb) white sugarpaste and colour it with black and blue paste food colourings to produce a marbled effect, as shown in step 2. Roll out the marble-effect sugarpaste and cover the fireplace. Using the same colour sugarpaste, cut panels and a mantelpiece, as shown in step 4. Make grooves in the panels with the tail-end of a paintbrush.

● Measure the width of the grate. Use a no. 3 piping tube (tip) and a little royal icing to pipe a guard for the front of the fire, as shown in step 6. Also pipe in detail on the small centre panel beneath the mantelpiece; paint over when dry to blend with the mantelpiece.

● Divide the remaining sugarpaste into small pieces and colour each piece differently. Model several jugs and pots of various colours, shapes and sizes. Dry them overnight if you wish to paint them as illustrated opposite. Attach to the mantelpiece with a little royal icing.

● Roll out a small piece of sugarpaste and cut out an oblong rug. Cut slits at both ends to represent the fringed edge. Pipe a greeting on the rug, if you wish, and leave to dry. Paint a pattern on the rug once the paste is dry.

● Make logs with small pieces of sugarpaste as shown in step 5.

● Trim the edge of the board with 1cm (½ in) wide ribbon.

EXPERT ADVICE
≈

Measure the fireplace carefully for the guard at the front of the grate before piping it onto waxed paper.

~ 1 ~

Cut the cake into three as shown. Cut an oblong hole 10cm (4 in) high, 11cm (4½ in) wide, 2cm (¾ in) deep in the largest piece, leaving 2.5cm (1 in) at the bottom and 3.5cm (1½ in) at the top. Build up both sides with 2cm (¾ in) deep oblongs of cake to the top of the hole.

~ 2 ~

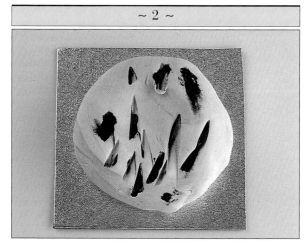

Colour the sugarpaste unevenly to resemble marble. Add a little black food colouring, knead it slightly, then add small dabs of blue and black. Knead again gently until a streaky or marbled effect is achieved. Then roll out the paste and use to cover the cake.

~ 5 ~

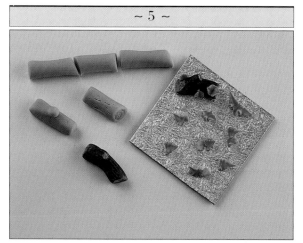

LOGS: use 125g (4 oz) brown sugarpaste. Roll 7.5mm (⅓ in) cylinders and cut 2.5 – 3cm (1 – 1½ in) lengths. Cut one end of each at an angle. Scratch wood marks with a cocktail stick. Paint ends cream and sides dark brown. Add stumps of branches. Place in grate when dry.

~ 6 ~

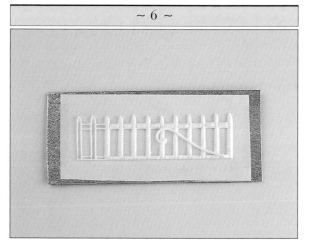

Using the template on page 70, a small amount of royal icing and a no. 3 piping tube (tip), pipe a guard to fit the front of the fireplace on waxed paper. Extend or reduce the guard as required by varying the number of rails. Leave to dry before attaching to the fireplace.

~ 3 ~

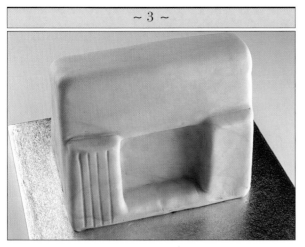

Cut two 5mm (¼ in) thick oblong panels of sugarpaste for either side of the fireplace, make grooves in both panels using the tail-end of a paintbrush.

~ 4 ~

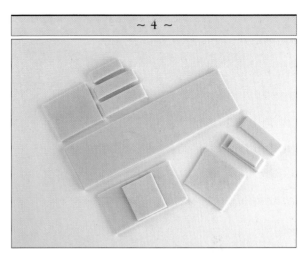

Cut a strip of sugarpaste for the mantelpiece; this should overlap both ends very slightly.

~ 7 ~

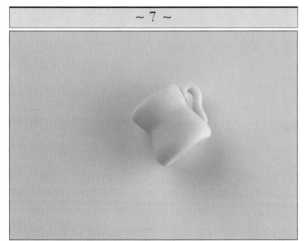

Model the jugs and pots in sugarpaste, using a ball modelling tool to hollow their tops. Vary the shapes, sizes and colours of the jugs and pots, ensuring none of them exceeds 4cm (1½ in) in height. When the sugarpaste is dry, paint the patterns of your choice on the jugs.

~ 8 ~

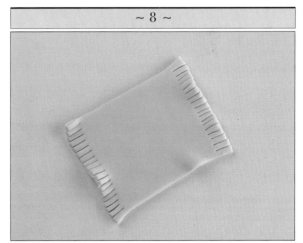

Rug: *roll out a 7.5 x 4.5cm (3 x 1¾ in) oblong of pink sugarpaste. Make 1cm (½ in) cuts into both ends to form a fringe. When attaching to board, lift fringe in places with the tip of a paintbrush. Paint pattern on rug when the sugarpaste has dried.*

WALKING BOOTS

2 x 13cm (5 in) basin Sponge Cakes,
see page 6
1 x 28 x 18cm (11 x 7 in) oblong Sponge Cake,
see page 6
strawberry jam (conserve), lemon curd or
Buttercream, see page 7
125ml (4 fl oz/½ cup) Royal Icing, see page 8
250ml (8 fl oz/1 cup) Apricot Glaze,
see page 8
1.25kg (2½ lb) sugarpaste
dark brown, Christmas red, melon yellow,
berry blue, mint green, tangerine, liquorice
black and grape violet paste food colours
gold lustre powder

EQUIPMENT
36cm (14 in) round cake board
no. 1 and 2 paintbrushes
plastic smoother
no. 1 and 1.5 piping tubes (tips)
ball modelling tool
cocktail sticks (toothpicks)
1.5m (1⅔ yd) of 1cm (½ in) wide fern green
ribbon

● Stand the basin cakes dome uppermost, then trim the top and sides to flatten and reduce the round effect at the toe, as shown in step 1.

● Using the template on page 71, cut four 10cm (4 in) diameter circles to form the heel. Stack two circles on top of each other. Cut a slight curve out of the back of the toe piece; this will allow the two circles to be tucked snugly behind, forming the heel.

● Hollow out a circle from the top layer of each heel, down to a depth of approximately 1cm (½ in), leaving a lip of 1cm (½ in) around the top edge, as shown in step 2.

● Sandwich the pieces of cake together with the filling of your choice and attach to the board with a little royal icing. Coat both boots with apricot glaze.

● Colour 1kg (2 lb) sugarpaste brown. Before covering the boots completely with sugarpaste, cut two strips of brown sugarpaste for the tongues, as shown in step 3, and lay them in place. Roll out the remaining sugarpaste and cover the boots, then quickly cut and fold back the flaps to reveal the tongues. Mark out lines around the heels and following the lines of the tongues, using the tail-end of a paintbrush.

● Jazz-up the walking boots by making a pair of socks, as shown in step 5, and paint them when the paste has dried.

● Pipe eyelets using a no. 1.5 piping tube (tip) and a little soft royal icing, see page 20. Pipe an oval with a line across the centre, filling in one half with royal icing.

● When the eyelets are dry, paint them with gold lustre powder which is mixed to a paste with a little water. Pipe in laces with a no. 2 piping tube (tip) and a little firmer royal icing.

● Coil the icing over itself to achieve a rope effect, as illustrated. Paint the laces with rainbow colours when dry.

● Make soles for the bottom of the boots using a thin roll of sugarpaste, as illustrated in step 6. Using a cocktail stick (toothpick) prick out lines to represent stitching, following the grooves made earlier around the heels and tongues.

● Decorate the board with green royal icing as shown, if liked, and trim the edge with ribbon.

PAINTING THE SOCKS

❖

Give the walking boots a colourful image by painting the socks to suit the recipient, using bright colours and a simple, bold pattern. Make the socks and leave the paste to dry completely before attempting to paint a pattern on it. When the royal icing has dried, the piped laces may also be painted to match the socks.

Boot tongue

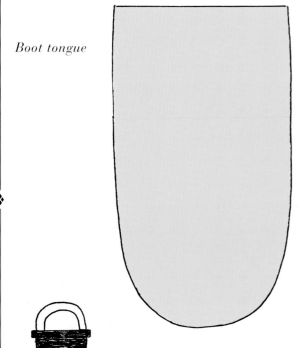

Eyelets

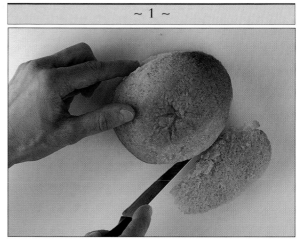

Trim the top and sides of the basin cakes to narrow and flatten the front of the boots slightly.

EXPERT ADVICE

≈

When impressing features into paste for novelty cakes, always work quickly before the sugarpaste dries, otherwise it will crack. For example, the lines and stitching must be marked on the boots before the paste dries.

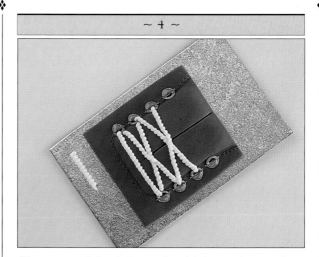

Use a no. 1.5 piping tube (tip) to pipe eyelets. Pipe an upright oval with a line across the middle and fill one half with icing. Use a no. 2 piping tube (tip) to pipe the laces and pipe a tight continuous coil for the best effect.

~ 2 ~

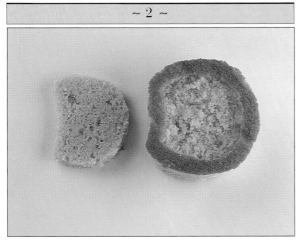

Cut a small curve out of the back of each toe piece, so that the heel circles sit neatly behind. Hollow out the tops of the heels leaving 1cm (½ in) clear around the edge.

~ 3 ~

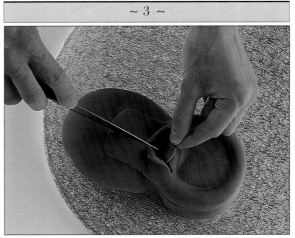

Cut a 10 x 5cm (4 x 2 in) piece of sugarpaste in the shape of a tongue. Attach it so that the rounded edge of the tongue protrudes by 1cm (½ in) over the heel piece. Cover the cake and immediately cut the sugarpaste in a T-shape to reveal the tongue. Curl the two side pieces back.

~ 5 ~

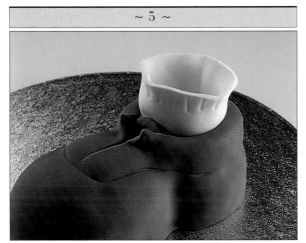

Cut a strip of sugarpaste, approximately 3.5 cm (1½ in) wide, attach around the top edge of the heel allowing it to sag slightly. Mark grooves in the strip to represent the ribbing of a sock.

~ 6 ~

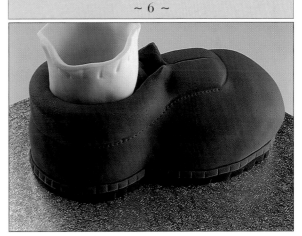

Roll a piece of black sugarpaste into a long sausage, approximately 5 – 7mm (¼ – ⅜ in) thick and attach around the base of the boots. Mark tread patterns using the tail-end of a paintbrush, tucking it underneath the sole of the boot and lifting it gently upwards.

TWO'S COMPANY

*T*his slightly different idea for a novelty cake is ideal for animal lovers and anyone who is interested in nature.

25cm (10 in) square Sponge Cake, see page 6
strawberry jam (conserve), lemon curd or
Buttercream, see page 7
125ml (4 fl oz/½ cup) Apricot Glaze,
see page 8
1kg (2 lb) sugarpaste
250g (8 oz) modelling paste
375ml (12 fl oz/1½ cups) Royal Icing,
see page 8
liquorice black, dark brown and berry blue
paste food colours
turquoise liquid food colour

E Q U I P M E N T
30cm (12 in) square cake board
no. 1, 2 and 3 paintbrushes
ball modelling tool
no. 0 and 1 piping tubes (tips)
1.25m (4 ft) of 1cm (½ in) wide blue ribbon

● Colour half of the royal icing blue and coat the edges of the cake board. The icing should be spread roughly to produce a watery image, as illustrated on page 24.

● On a separate board, turn the cake upside down and using the template on page 71, cut out the shape of the iceberg. Build up a rough but structured shape using the sponge cake trimmings, as shown in step 1.

● Cut and sandwich the cake with the filling of your choice, then coat with apricot glaze. Roll out 750g (1½ lb) of sugarpaste a little thicker than usual, approximately 5mm (¼ in) thick – this will allow ample thickness for moulding the paste into iceberg peaks. Cover the iceberg, but do not attach it to the coated board yet.

● To give the iceberg texture, make grooves and dents in the sugarpaste using the tail-end of a paintbrush and a tapered knife blade. Use your fingers to draw up the icing to form ice walls and ice slides, as illustrated in step 2. Model some mini icebergs to scatter on the top of the large iceberg and in the sea. The more uneven the appearance the better.

● Carefully transfer the iceberg to the iced board, attaching it with a little royal icing.

● Pipe the wave pattern around the sides of the iceberg using a greaseproof (parchment) paper piping bag and some blue royal icing. Snip the end off of the piping bag to leave a hole the size of a no. 3 piping tube (tip). The wave pattern is illustrated in step 3.

● Finally, to give the iceberg more depth, paint a little grey food colouring into some of the crevices and grooves.

● Knead 125g (4 oz) each of modelling paste and sugarpaste together and use to model the seals. Begin by moulding the basic shape, as shown in the diagram on page 24. Mark lines on the flippers with a knife and quickly make holes for the eyes and nose before the paste dries.

● Make up a brushing solution of royal icing by adding water to a teaspoon of royal icing, mixing it until it resembles a thin paste. Colour

---

EXPERT ADVICE
≈

When modelling animals of any kind, have a book or photograph to refer to, because it is amazing how many tiny details you miss working from memory.

half of the icing grey and, using a no. 2 paintbrush, brush the icing over the seals to create a textured appearance. When the seals are dry, brush on some patches of darker grey and cream to give them a little more depth and variance, as shown in step 4.

● Pipe in the eyes with a little black royal icing and a no. 1 piping tube (tip). Paint fine dark lines around the eyes, paint in the eyebrows and any other remaining details to give better definition to the features. Pipe on the whiskers with a no. 0 piping tube (tip) and a little grey royal icing.

● Place the seals on the iceberg cake and trim the edge of the board with ribbon.

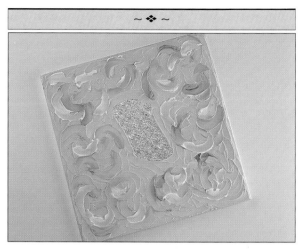

Coat the cake board by applying blue royal icing with a swirling motion. Cover up to 7.5cm (3 in) in from the edge. Also add swirls of a darker blue and white royal icing for a better effect.

EXPERT ADVICE

≈

Modelling paste dries out much quicker than sugarpaste, so work as quickly as you can, but don't panic!

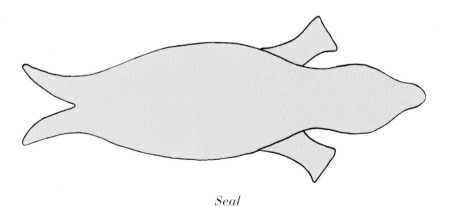

Seal

~ 1 ~

Cut the basic shape of the iceberg using the template on page 71, building up an uneven but structured shape with the off-cuts of sponge cake.

~ 2 ~

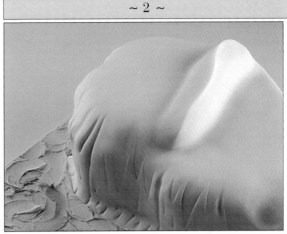

When coated with sugarpaste, add texture to the iceberg by using the tail-end of a paintbrush and the tip of a tapered bladed knife to mark grooves in the sides. Draw the icing up with your fingers to form ice walls.

~ 3 ~

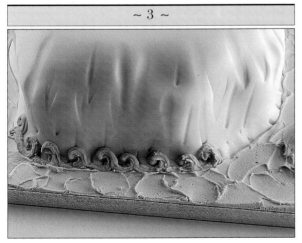

Use some blue royal icing in a greaseproof paper piping bag to pipe a wave pattern around the bottom edge of the iceberg. There is no need to fit a piping tube (tip) in the bag – snip the point off with scissors. When the waves are dry, lightly brush their crests with white royal icing.

~ 4 ~

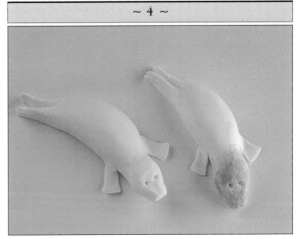

Make the basic shape for the seal, tapering it at both ends. Mark the eyes, nose and flippers and leave to dry. When dry, brush with a royal icing solution to give a textured effect. When dry again, paint on additional markings in cream or darker grey and pipe on whiskers.

SLEEPING BEAUTY

*28cm (11 in) x 18cm (7 in) oblong Sponge
Cake, see page 6
strawberry jam (conserve), lemon curd or
Buttercream, see page 7
250ml (8 fl oz/1 cup) Royal Icing, see page 8
125ml (4 fl oz/½ cup) Apricot Glaze,
see page 8
1kg (2 lb) sugarpaste
raspberry red liquid food colouring
250g (8 oz) modelling paste
berry blue, mint green, dark brown and
melon yellow paste food colourings
mango and pink dusting powder
(petal dust/blossom tint)
4 x 15cm (6 in) long pink and white striped
candy sticks or dowels*

EQUIPMENT

*30cm (12 in) square cake board
no. 1 and 2 paintbrushes
plastic smoother
no. 2 and 3 piping tubes (tips)
waxed paper
16 x 23cm (6½ x 9 in) piece of lace or netting
small pieces of foam
1.25m (4 ft) of 1cm (½ in) wide pink ribbon*

● Cut the cake into three pieces across the width: two pieces should be 11 x 18cm (4½ x 7 in) and one piece 5 x 18cm (2 x 7 in), the latter will be the pillow. Sandwich the pieces of cake together with the filling of your choice, then attach to the board with a little royal icing. Coat with apricot glaze.

● Roll out half the sugarpaste thinly and cover the base of the bed. Cover the pillow separately. Pipe a frill around the edge of the pillow using a no. 57 petal piping tube (tip) and a little pink royal icing. Shake the tube (tip), gently, from side to side as you pipe to produce a gathered effect as illustrated on page 11.

● Build up the shape of the body under the sheets with sponge cake, as illustrated in step 2. Model arms and legs using sugarpaste. Model the head as shown in step 3. When dry, paint on the eyes and eyebrows and blush the cheeks with pink dusting powder (petal dust/blossom tint).

● Colour 250g (8 oz) sugarpaste pink. Roll this out to make the bed cover, as illustrated in step 4, adding a border of white sugarpaste. Paint the darker pink and yellow design on the bed cover using a fine paintbrush and food colourings before folding back the white sugarpaste edge. Alternatively, the cover may be left plain pink.

● Pipe a frill edge around the cover as for the pillow once it is in position on the bed. Use a no. 3 piping tube (tip) to pipe the edging around the bottom of the cake.

● Knead equal quantities of sugarpaste and modelling paste together and use to mould Sleeping Beauty's head as shown in step 3.

● Model the Prince's body out of blue modelling paste as illustrated on pages 13 and 29. Using a no. 3 piping tube (tip) and a little royal icing, pipe a sword onto waxed paper. Use the diagram on page 71 as a guide or trace it to make a template if you are nervous about piping the shape freehand. Pipe hair with a no. 2 piping tube (tip). Use small pieces of foam to support the Prince's body while it dries.

● To create the four-poster bed effect, use either four pink and white striped candy sticks or four pieces of dowel. Sink the four candy stick posts or dowels carefully into the cake corners, not too close to the edge or the

sugarpaste will crack. Put a little dab of icing on the top of each post and drape a piece of lace or net curtain over the top to represent the canopy.

● Dowels may be decorated with trailing roses, stems and leaves. Small balls of leftover paste may be stuck on the top of the dowels and painted with silver food colouring.

● Attach the 1cm (½ in) wide pink ribbon around the edge of the board with a little glue. The decoration may be completed by colouring a small piece of sugarpaste yellow and using it to make a small circular rug. Mark the rug with a round cutter which is slightly smaller than the paste to make a fringe effect around the edge. Piped flowers and a greeting may be added to the rug.

~ 1 ~

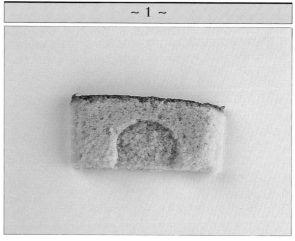

Trim a little cake off at both ends of the pillow to achieve a sloping effect. Carve a small hollow in the centre of the pillow to support the head.

~ ❖ ~

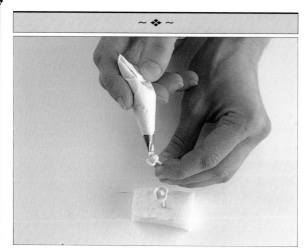

Roses *Use a no. 57 petal piping tube. Grease the tip of a cocktail stick (toothpick) with white vegetable fat. With the narrow end of the tube tip upwards, pipe a cone of icing on the stick for a bud. Pipe 3 overlapping petals to complete the rose. Let dry on the stick.*

~ 4 ~

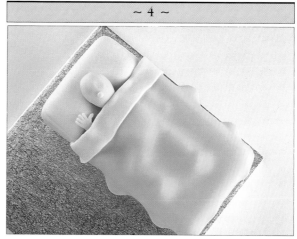

Roll out the pink sugarpaste large enough to slightly overlap the bed. Cut to shape with a wavy line to soften the edge. Place a strip of white sugarpaste 3cm (1¼ in) in width along the top edge to represent a sheet; fold the top edge over and underneath the bottom cover to finish.

~ 2 ~

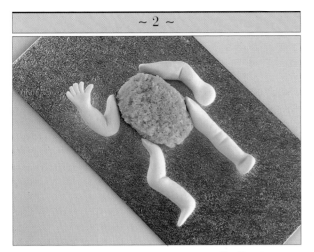

Shape a piece of cake, rounding off all edges, to represent a body under the sheets.

~ 3 ~

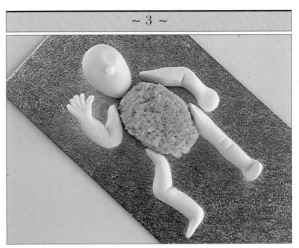

Take a plum-sized piece of flesh-coloured sugarpaste and modelling paste kneaded together. Shape it into an oval to represent a head, making almond-shaped holes for the eyes before it dries. Attach the nose. Leave to dry before painting features.

~ 5 ~

Model the Prince's body, arms, legs and head as illustrated. Leave the legs to dry separately in a kneeling position. If you use cocktail sticks (toothpicks) to strengthen and support the Prince, ensure that everyone knows that they are there.

~ 6 ~

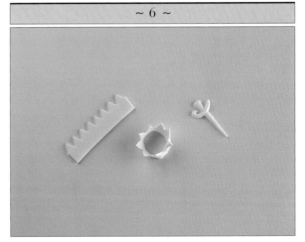

Pipe a sword onto waxed paper with a little royal icing and a no. 3 piping tube (tip). For the crown, roll out a 4 x 1.5cm (1¾ x ¾ in) strip of modelling paste and cut one edge in a zig-zag pattern. Stick the ends together to form the crown.

HOT GOSSIP

25cm (10 in) square Sponge Cake, page 6
strawberry jam (conserve), lemon curd or
Buttercream, see page 7
185ml (6 fl oz/¾ cup) Apricot Glaze, see page 8
1kg (2 lb) sugarpaste
125ml (4 fl oz/½ cup) Royal Icing,
see page 8
cornflour (cornstarch)
icing (confectioners') sugar
Christmas red and liquorice black paste
food colourings
silver food colouring
E Q U I P M E N T
30cm (12 in) round cake board
no. 1 and 3 piping tubes (tips)
plastic smoother
1m (1 yd) of 1cm (½ in) wide red ribbon

● Cut the cake as shown in the step-by-step photographs. Cut off a 7cm (3 in) strip and reserve it for the handpiece. Cut the remaining cake in half widthways to give two oblongs each measuring 25 x 7cm (10 x 3 in). Hold one piece on its side and slice it lengthways at a slant to shape the front of the telephone. Cut from about 7cm (3 in) from the top edge of one end

down to the bottom of the cake at the opposite end.
● Cut curved sections from the sides of the slanting cake, then place it on top of the complete oblong.
● Carve the handset from the reserved strip of cake. Both ends of the handset should be rounded to represent the mouth and earpieces. Cut a small curved piece of cake from the underside of the handset so that it curves slightly in the middle.
● Sandwich the cake together with the filling of your choice and attach it to the board with a little royal icing. Coat with apricot glaze.
● Reserve a small amount of sugarpaste for the dial and curly wire, then colour the remaining sugarpaste red. Roll out the red sugarpaste and cover the telephone and handset separately. Smooth the paste neatly around and over the pieces of cake, gently easing out creases.
● Make a dial or buttons out of white sugarpaste, as shown in step 4, using the diagrams on page 32 as a guide. Paint the upper piece of the dial, which has finger holes, with silver food colouring, if liked. Pipe a message or the recipient's age in the centre of the dial. Pipe numbers on the dial or buttons using a no. 1 piping tube (tip) and a little black royal icing.
● To make the curly wire which connects the handset to the telephone, colour a small piece of sugarpaste black and roll it into a long 'worm'. Then curl it as shown in the photograph on page 32. Attach the wire to the telephone and the handset by painting it with a little water.
● Trim the edge of the board with the 1cm (½ in) wide red ribbon.

EXPERT ADVICE
≈

If the bottom edge of your telephone cake is not as neat as you hoped, colour a small amount of royal icing red and use a no. 3 piping tube (tip) to pipe a row of plain shells around the base of the telephone to conceal the edge of the sugarpaste.

EXPERT ADVICE

≈

If you have problems shaping the coiled paste to represent the telephone wire, dust a piece of dowel lightly with cornflour (cornstarch) and coil the paste around it. Leave to dry, then carefully slide the coiled paste off the dowel.

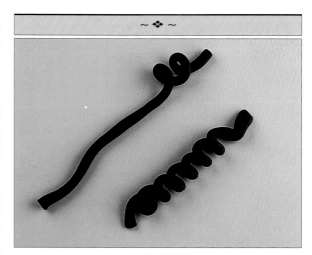

Roll a piece of black sugarpaste into a long thin worm. Roll it over itself several times to form a coil, as illustrated.

Telephone buttons

Telephone dial

0	1	2	✳
3	4	5	∠R
6	7	8	M
9	B T	#	S

~ 1 ~

Cut a 7cm (3 in) strip off the cake. Cut the remaining cake in half so that you have two 18 x 12.5cm (7 x 5 in) pieces. Cut the top off one piece at a slant: cut into the cake slightly about 7cm (3 in) from one end. Turn it on its side and cut to the bottom at the opposite end.

~ 2 ~

Cut a curve out of each side of the slanting rectangle of cake so that it is wider at the bottom than the top.

~ 3 ~

Place the slanting cake on top of the complete rectangle. Carve a handset from the 7cm (3 in) strip of cake, rounding off all the edges as much as possible.

~ 4 ~

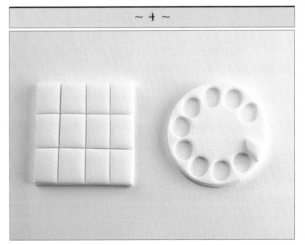

For a dial, roll sugarpaste thinly and cut out two 7.5cm (3 in) circles. Cut holes in one with the wide end of a piping tube (tip). Dampen the complete circle and position the dial on top. For buttons, cut a 7.5cm (3 in) square of thick sugarpaste and mark lines with a sharp knife.

SOFA MICE

*A*fter seeing this cake someone asked me, in all seriousness, if I could re-upholster a chair for them!

25cm (10 in) square Sponge Cake, see page 6
strawberry jam (conserve), lemon curd or
Buttercream, see page 7
250ml (8 fl oz/1 cup) Apricot Glaze,
see page 8
1kg (2 lb) sugarpaste
500g (1 lb) modelling paste
125ml (4 fl oz/½ cup) Royal Icing, see page 8
dark brown, liquorice black, mint green,
blueberry, melon yellow and Christmas red
paste food colourings
turquoise, cream and raspberry red liquid
food colourings
peach and pink dusting powder
(petal dust/blossom tint)

EQUIPMENT
36cm (14 in) square cake board
plastic smoother
cocktail stick (toothpick)
ball modelling tool
no. 0 or 1 and 3 paintbrushes
no. 3 piping tube (tip)
1.5m (1⅔ yd) of 1cm (½ in) wide pink or
peach ribbon

EXPERT ADVICE
≈

It is fun giving each mouse a slightly different expression – with a little imagination, you will be amazed just how cheeky or individual they can become.

- Cut the cake into three pieces: 15cm (6 in), 6cm (2½ in) and 3cm (1½ in). Stand the largest piece on end, longest side to the the board, and shape the top to whichever style you prefer for the back of the sofa. Round off the edges as shown on page 36.

- Cut the 25 x 2.5cm (10 x 1 in) strip of cake in half to make the arms of the sofa. Trim off any rough sides or edges and shape the ends, as shown in step 1. The arms should be slightly higher than the seat; if they are not, build them up by placing a small piece of sponge or sugarpaste underneath.

- Sandwich the cake with the filling of your choice. Stick the individual pieces to each other with a little royal icing and to the board with a little royal icing, then coat with apricot glaze.

- Colour the sugarpaste with a little cream and a little raspberry red food colouring. Roll out to approximately 5mm (¼ in) thick and cover the cake, as illustrated in step 3. Leave to dry for 24 hours.

- Colour a small piece of modelling paste a darker pink, roll out and make a frill, as shown on page 11. Attach the frill to the bottom edge of the sofa as shown in step 4.

- Using a no. 3 piping tube (tip) and a little pink royal icing, pipe single lines of shells along the outside edge of each arm, along the top two edges of the back of the sofa and around the bottom of the cake, just above the frill.

- Paint on a design of your choice, using a fine paintbrush, no. 0 or 1, and a little food colouring, as shown in step 5.

- Colour the remaining modelling paste light brown with a hint of peach and model the mice following the instructions on pages 12 – 13 and as illustrated in step 6. Take five small pieces of sugarpaste and colour each of them differently:

red, blue, green, yellow and orange for modelling the wellington boots, as shown.

● Colour a piece of sugarpaste dark brown and make noses for the mice. Paint on the eyes and mouth when dry.

● Arrange the mice on the sofa. Make a rug to decorate the board and leave to dry before painting a pattern on it and adding a piped or painted greeting. Trim the board edge with ribbon.

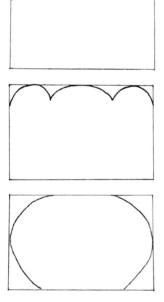

Sofa back variations

EXPERT ADVICE

≈

Always add colour to paste in minute amounts as more can easily be added once the first amount has been kneaded in. Remember that the colours normally dry to a more intense shade than they appear when the paste is wet.

~ 1 ~

Cut the pieces of cake, round off the ends of the arms and neaten top edges.

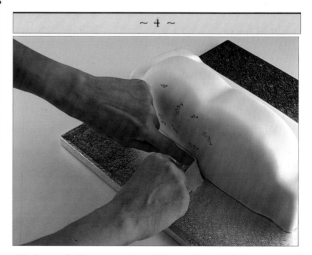

~ 4 ~

Make a frill, see page 11, and attach it around the bottom edge by dampening the cake using a paintbrush and a little water.

~ 2 ~

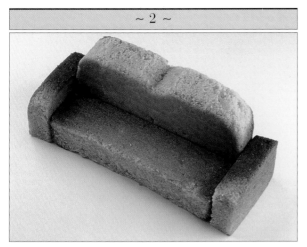

Assemble the sofa as shown, attaching each piece to the board with a little royal icing. Begin with the seat, then the carved back and finally the arms. Attach the pieces to each other with a little royal icing.

~ 3 ~

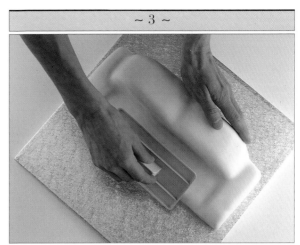

Roll the sugarpaste out to at least twice the width and one-and-a-half times the length of the sofa. Lay the paste over the sofa, gently easing it into every corner. Work carefully into the seat and down the back of the sofa. Use a plastic smoother to give a smooth finish.

~ 5 ~

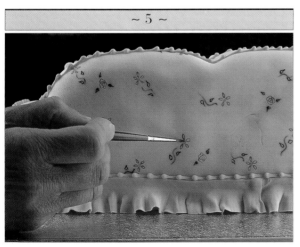

Use a fine paintbrush to paint flowers or any other design you have chosen for the sofa. Always paint in a random fashion so as to avoid a very square or uniform look.

~ 6 ~

The mice can be made in advance, if you like, and stored in an airtight container for several days.

JOLLY LION

25cm (10 in) square Sponge Cake, see page 6
20cm (8 in) square Sponge Cake, see page 6
apricot jam (conserve), lemon curd or
Buttercream, see page 7, optional
a little Royal Icing, see page 8
250ml (8 fl oz/1 cup) Apricot Glaze,
see page 8
1.5kg (3 lb) sugarpaste
dark brown, liquorice black, melon yellow,
chestnut brown and peach paste food
colourings
cream liquid food colouring
mango dusting powder (petal dust/blossom tint)

EQUIPMENT

30cm (12 in) round cake board
no. 1, 2 and 3 paintbrushes
ball modelling tool
plastic smoother
1.25m (4ft) of 1cm (½ in) wide yellow ribbon

● Using the templates on page 40, cut both sponges to shape.

● Cut and sandwich the cakes, if liked, with the filling of your choice. Build up the facial features with pieces of cake as illustrated in step 1. Attach each piece with a little apricot jam or royal icing.

● Attach the base cake to the board with a little royal icing and attach the face cake to the top of the base cake in the same way. Coat both cakes with a layer of apricot glaze.

● Colour 750g (1½ lb) sugarpaste with cream, yellow and brown paste food colourings to achieve a rich golden colour. Roll out the sugarpaste to 5mm (¼ in) thick and cover the two cakes completely. Cut out two 2.5cm (1 in) ovals of sugarpaste, of a similar thickness, for the lion's eyes. Leave to dry, then paint as shown in step 2.

● Before the sugarpaste coating dries, make indentations for the nostrils using the ball modelling tool. Mark out the lion's mouth using the tail-end of a paintbrush. Model the eyelids as shown in step 3.

● Cut the remaining sugarpaste into five portions and colour each piece differently: cream, golden yellow, dark cream, mid-brown and fawn. Golden yellow is made by kneading melon yellow and cream into the sugarpaste. Make several rolls of sugarpaste, tapering them at one end, as shown in step 5. Twist and curl some pieces when attaching them to the cake. Frame the entire lion's head, building up a thick mane in a variety of gold and brown tones.

● To give the face a furry, textured look, brush on a little fawn-coloured royal icing, mixed to a brushing consistency with a little water. Apply to the face with a no. 2 or 3 paintbrush. Make the eyebrows more pronounced by brushing on a little extra royal icing. Remember that fur does not lie in straight lines; brush outwards and upwards across the cheeks and from the centre outwards on both sides of the nose.

● Model a pair of ears from two small balls of sugarpaste, flattened and indented in the centre as shown in step 4. Paint on any remaining details such as the mouth, rims of the eyes and the shading of the nostrils. Brush the insides of the ears with pale peach dusting powder (petal dust/blossom tint).

● Trim the board edge with ribbon.

Lion's head templates
Enlarge by 244 per cent on a photocopier

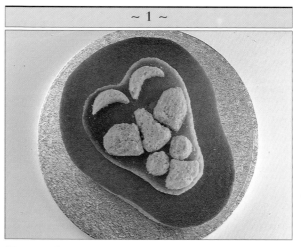

~ 1 ~

Trace the two templates and enlarge on a photocopier. Use to accurately and smoothly cut the base cake and face shapes for the lion's head. Using leftover pieces of cake, build up the lion's muzzle, nose and mouth. Carve oval-shaped pieces for the cheeks and half-moons for the eyebrows. Place two small circles beneath the nose and a shaped semi-circle for the chin. If you run short of cake, use a little sugarpaste to build the features. When the features are fixed the cake is ready for coating with sugarpaste.

EXPERT ADVICE

≈

It is not difficult to make a template. Begin by drawing a basic outline with good definition, then reduce or enlarge it on a photocopier to the size required for the cake. Cut the shape out and use it as a template for carving a shape in sponge cake.

~ 2 ~

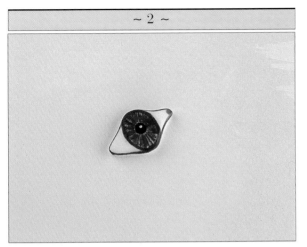

Cut almond-shaped eyes out of a piece of sugar-paste. Attach to the face using a paintbrush and a little water. Leave to dry before painting on detail as shown here on a single cut-out eye.

~ 3 ~

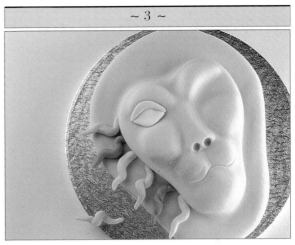

Model eyelids by rolling two thin sausages of sugarpaste and attaching them above the eyes, following the curve of the eyeball.

~ 4 ~

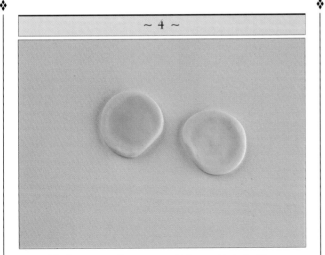

Mould the ears from two 2.5cm (1 in) diameter circles, squashing them and modelling a rim around the edge. Attach with a little water.

~ 5 ~

Using a paintbrush and mango dusting powder, apply a little colour to the bridge of the nose, upper cheekbones and chin. Taper the rolls for the mane at one end, curl some, but not all. Vary the colours of sugarpaste to give depth. Ensure the mane is full, without any gaps.

GET WELL SOON

*S*end a Get Well cake instead of a card to someone who has spent a while in hospital.

20cm (8 in) square Sponge Cake, see page 6
strawberry jam (conserve), lemon curd or
Buttercream, see page 7
125ml (4 fl oz/½ cup) Apricot Glaze,
see page 8
1kg (2 lb) sugarpaste
125g (4 oz) modelling paste
250ml (8 fl oz/1 cup) Royal Icing, see page 8
mint green, liquorice black, dark brown and
tangerine paste food colourings
raspberry pink liquid food colouring
silver lustre powder
EQUIPMENT
25cm (10 in) square cake board
no. 2 and 4 piping tubes (tips)
no. 2 and 4 paintbrushes
plastic smoother
waxed paper
1m (1 yd) of 1cm (½ in) wide green ribbon

● Slice the sponge in half and sandwich the two layers together with the filling of your choice. Coat the cake with apricot glaze.

● Roll out half the sugarpaste to 5mm (¼ in) thick and cover the cake.

● Colour 125g (4 oz) sugarpaste flesh colour, kneading in a little tangerine and pink paste colouring. Model the patient's body, arms, legs and head out of sugarpaste as shown in step 2, remembering that it will all be covered, except for the location of the operation and the head. The head should be oval in shape and allowed to dry before the features are painted.

● Knead 125g (4 oz) each of sugarpaste and modelling paste together, then colour the paste bright green. Roll out thinly and cut into strips, as shown in step 2. Lay the strips across the patient, leaving a space for the location of the operation. Lay the strips both horizontally and vertically.

● Colour a small piece of sugarpaste grey and model a cylinder shape, as shown, to stand beside the operating table. When dry paint on O2 or another chemical symbol for the gas of your choice.

● Using the diagrams on pages 44 and 45 as a guide, pipe some surgical instruments onto waxed paper with a no. 2 piping tube (tip) and a little royal icing, as shown in step 3. Leave to dry for at least 24 hours. When dry paint with moistened silver lustre powder.

● Paint the location of the operation yellow and paint a broken line to represent the planned incision. Roll out a little white sugarpaste thinly and cut into 1cm (½ in) squares to represent swabs. Cut a slightly larger oblong to represent a chart, to hang at the bottom of the bed.

● Using a no. 4 piping tube (tip) pipe in four bed posts, as shown, painting them with moistened silver lustre powder when dry. Trim the edge of the board with 1cm (½ in) wide green ribbon.

~ 1 ~

Roll out half the sugarpaste to one-and-a-half times the length and width of the cake. Lift the paste on a rolling pin and cover the cake. Mould it neatly in place, lifting out any creases with one hand, then smooth it with a plastic smoother.

~ 2 ~

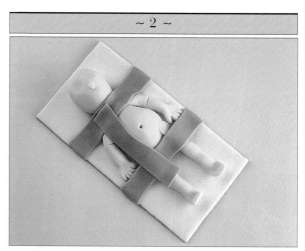

Make a body, two arms, two legs and a head out of flesh-coloured sugarpaste. The shapes of the arms and legs only need to be basic, because they will be covered. Model a button nose and attach it to the face. Roll out green-coloured paste of equal quantities of sugarpaste and modelling paste kneaded together until thin. Cut into 1.5cm (¾ in) wide strips. Lay the strips in both directions across the patient.

~ 3 ~

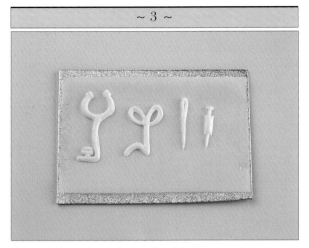

Using a no. 2 piping tube (tip), pipe the shapes of various surgical instruments onto waxed paper. Use the diagrams on page 44 as a guide or trace them to make accurate templates. Leave to dry for at least 24 hours before painting with silver lustre powder moistened with a hint of water.

~ 4 ~

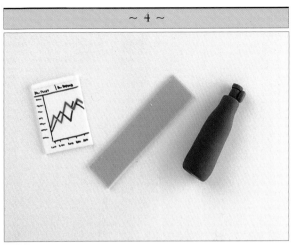

Make a chart from a piece of sugarpaste, leave it to dry, then paint on erratic red and blue lines and other details in black. Paint the top edge of the chart with moistened silver lustre powder. Cut a strip of green paste to make the patient's cap. Fit it around the head and trim it neatly. Roll a cylinder of grey sugarpaste to represent an oxygen tank, shaping the top as shown. The cylinder is labelled with O2 on the side and it is placed on the cake board beside the bed. Complete the oxygen equipment by attaching a long thin sausage of paste with an oxygen mask attached on the end. The top of the cylinder and the oxygen mask are both painted with silver lustre powder moistened with a hint of water.

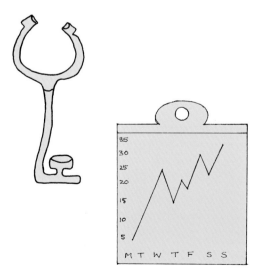

LITTLE BROWN TEAPOT

13cm (5 in) basin Sponge Cake, see page 6
15cm (6 in) square Sponge Cake, see page 6
strawberry jam (conserve), lemon curd or
Buttercream, see page 7
250ml (8 fl oz/1 cup) Apricot Glaze,
see page 8
750g (1½ lb) sugarpaste
250g (½ lb) modelling paste
125ml (4 fl oz/½ cup) Royal Icing, see page 8
dark brown, mint green and blueberry paste
food colourings
raspberry pink and cream liquid food
colourings
gold lustre dusting powder
(petal dust/blossom tint)

EQUIPMENT
25cm (10 in) square cake board
no. 1 paintbrush
no. 1 piping tube (tip)
ball modelling tool
small pieces of foam
cocktail sticks (toothpicks)
1.25m (4 ft) of 1cm (½ in) wide yellow ribbon

The handle and spout have to be made in advance and allowed to dry for at least 48 hours, the longer the better, so make these first. Knead a piece of sugarpaste the size of a large plum with a similar-sized piece of modelling paste. Colour the paste dark brown. Do not knead the colour thoroughly into the paste; leave it part-mixed to achieve a mottled or marbled effect.

Divide the paste in half. Roll both pieces into sausage shapes then model a spout and handle, as shown in the photograph of the finished

cake, opposite. Leave on a board to dry.

Before covering and decorating the cake, the board may be decorated with a royal icing doiley if liked. Using white royal icing and a no. 1 piping tube (tip), pipe a continuous line of icing in a roughly circular shape, as shown in the photograph of the finished cake. This type of piping is known as cornelli work, taking a line for a walk or scribbling. The trick is to keep the line of icing unbroken and curling around upon itself until the area for decoration is completely filled. Neaten the edge of the work by piping small lace shapes. Leave to dry.

Stand the basin cake dome uppermost. Round off the bottom edge, as shown in step 1.

Using the template on page 49, cut two 8cm (3 in) diameter circles from the square sponge. Trim one circle to a depth of 1cm (½ in) and attach it beneath the dome with a little royal icing to make the base of the teapot. Carve out a hollow from the centre of the second circle, so that it fits snugly on top of the dome, as illustrated in step 2.

Assemble all the pieces of cake, attaching them to each other with a little royal icing, and fix the assembled cake to the board with a little royal icing.

Colour the sugarpaste dark brown. Do not knead the colour thoroughly into the paste, leave it partly kneaded to give a mottled or marbled effect. Coat the cake with apricot glaze. Roll out the brown sugarpaste to 5mm (¼ in) thick and cover cake. Gently ease the sugarpaste into the shape of the cake, carefully lifting out any folds with one hand as you mould the paste onto the cake with the other hand.

Roll out a thin band of modelling paste and cut it into a neat 3.5cm (1½ in) wide strip. Trim

this to fit around the teapot, just below the top sponge circle, then dampen the cake and press the modelling paste in place. Leave to dry.

● When dry, paint a pattern on the strip. I have chosen pink rosebuds with blue detail, as shown in step 4, but you can vary this, making it traditional or contemporary, delicate or bright and bold to suit the recipient.

● Pipe beading (small shells) along the top and bottom edge of the patterned strip, with a no. 1 piping tube (tip) and a little royal icing. Paint beading with moistened gold lustre powder when dry.

● Attach the handle and spout using a little royal icing. Insert cocktail sticks (toothpicks) into the spout and handle, then push them into the pot to provide more support. Use pieces of foam to support the spout and handle until the icing has dried. Make sure that everyone knows that there are cocktail sticks (toothpicks) in the cake.

● Trim the edge of the board with 1cm (½ in) wide yellow ribbon or a suitable colour to match the decoration on the teapot.

EXPERT ADVICE
≈

If you intend using cocktail sticks (toothpicks) to support an object or figure on the finished cake, make the holes in the sugarpaste before the paste dries. Use a cocktail stick to do this, taking care to put them in the correct position. Then, when the paste has dried, the sticks can be inserted easily when assembling the cake.

~ 1 ~

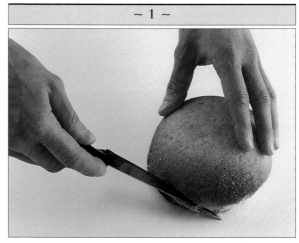

Trim off any square edges from around the base of the dome, holding the knife at an angle with the point facing the base of the cake. Smooth off to produce a rounded effect, as illustrated.

~ 3 ~

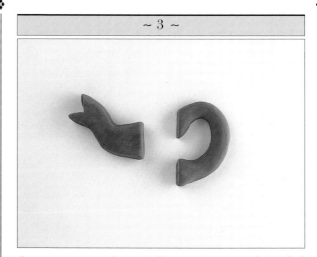

Sugarpaste and modelling paste are kneaded together for handle and spout. Roll two sausages 2cm (¾ in) thick, bend and mould to shape. Support with foam until dry. Attach to the teapot with royal icing and cocktail sticks (toothpicks) for support.

~ 2 ~

Trim an 8cm (3 in) circle of cake to 1cm (½ in) deep and place under the cake as shown. Carve a gently curving hollow out of a second 8cm (3 in) circle to fit on top of the dome as a lid.

Template for base and lid

~ 4 ~

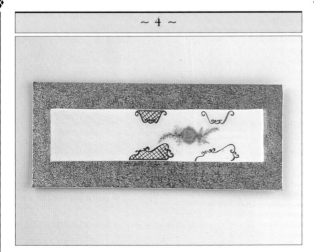

Use a fine no. 1 paintbrush and a little food colouring to paint the pattern of your choice onto the decorative band on the teapot. The band is positioned on the teapot and allowed to dry before the pattern is painted on; the strip of paste used here illustrates the technique.

EXPERT ADVICE

≈

The Little Brown Teapot is the ideal birthday cake for an elderly relative but it can be brightened up to make a colourful novelty cake. Cover the cake with strong-coloured paste, such as red, yellow or green, and apply a contemporary pattern to the band of white paste. Complement a brightly coloured cake by cutting out and painting a circle of sugarpaste to put underneath it on the board instead of piping the delicate base used for the traditional teapot.

HANG-GLIDER

*W*hat a wonderful way to beat traffic jams! Before starting this cake note that the wings have to be made first – at least four days in advance – to allow them to dry out thoroughly before they are placed on the cake.

185g (6 oz) modelling paste
20cm (8 in) square Sponge Cake, see page 6
strawberry jam (conserve), lemon curd or
Buttercream, see page 7
250ml (8 fl oz/1 cup) Royal Icing, see page 8
125ml (4 fl oz/½ cup) Apricot Glaze,
see page 8
500g (1 lb) sugarpaste
Christmas red, Christmas green, berry blue,
melon yellow, liquorice black, dark brown,
holly green and tangerine paste food colourings

E Q U I P M E N T
25cm (10 in) square cake board
no. 2 and 3 piping tubes (tips)
no. 1 and 2 paintbrushes
pieces of foam
plastic smoother
waxed paper
1m (1yd) of 1cm (½ in) wide green ribbon

● Make the wings for the hang-glider at least four days before you need them. Roll out the modelling paste to 3mm (⅛ in) thick and use the template on page 52 to cut out a pair of wings, as shown in step 1. Leave to dry.

● Slice the cake into two layers and sandwich with the filling of your choice. Attach to the board with a little royal icing, then coat with apricot glaze.

● Colour the sugarpaste evenly pale green, then partly knead in a little more colouring to produce a mottled effect. Roll out the sugarpaste to 5mm (¼ in) thick and cover the cake.

● Trace the sheep templates on page 52. Cover with waxed paper and pipe the sheep with a no. 2 piping tube (tip) and soft, but not runny, royal icing.

● Model the flying figure out of sugarpaste, as shown in step 3.

● Pipe the handbars for the hang-glider using royal icing and a no. 3 piping tube (tip), as shown in step 5.

● When the wings are completely dry, paint them using bright colours as shown in step 1.

● Place the figure on top of the cake and attach the wings with a little royal icing. Support the wings with pieces of foam until the icing is dry.

● Colour some royal icing green and stipple it on top of the cake to produce a grass effect, holding a paintbrush vertical to the surface and dabbing the icing gently.

● Paint the details on the sheep and attach to the top of the cake with a little royal icing. Stipple grass on the board around the bottom edge of the cake and trim with 1cm (½ in) wide green ribbon.

EXPERT ADVICE
≈

When making items such as the sheep, it is a good idea to make several more than you need while you have the templates in place and the icing mixed. This allows for any breakages which may happen later as you add the finishing touches or when handling and applying the pieces to the cake.

Wings

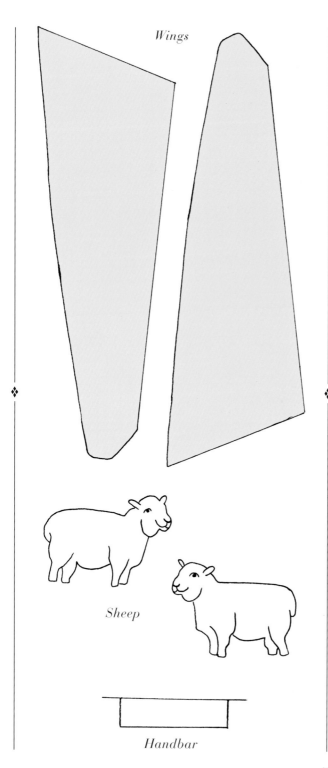

Sheep

Handbar

~ 1 ~

Use modelling paste for the wings. Cut neatly and clearly around the wings template with a sharp knife. Leave on a hard flat surface to dry for at least four days. Turn the wings over after two days. When dry, paint with vivid colours as shown.

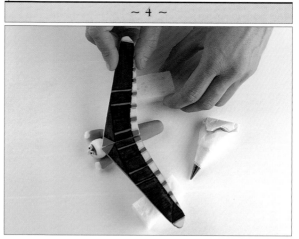

~ 4 ~

When the wings are thoroughly dry, stick them together with a little royal icing. Tilt both wings slightly upwards and support them with pieces of foam until the icing is dry. Attach to the figure and support with foam for at least 24 hours, until dry.

~ 2 ~

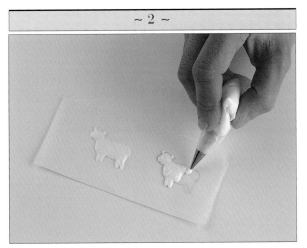

Trace the sheep templates on page 52 and lay waxed paper over them. Mix a little white royal icing to the consistency of yogurt. Use a no. 2 piping tube (tip) and the soft icing to fill the sheep templates. Pipe roughly to produce a wool-like result.

~ 3 ~

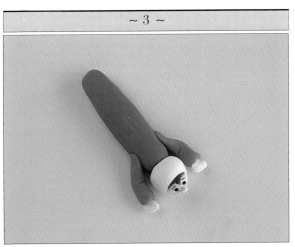

Roll a plum-sized piece of blue sugarpaste into a tapered sausage. Model a white helmet and carve a circle from the front: replace it with flesh-coloured paste; dry, then paint. Model tapered red arms, with holes for hands. Attach flesh-coloured hands with water.

~ 5 ~

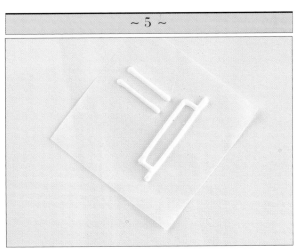

Measure the space between the wings and the cake, then pipe two vertical bars with a no. 3 piping tube (tip) and a little royal icing onto waxed paper. Also pipe a double horizontal bar which is long enough to protrude beyond both sides of the figure's hands.

~ 6 ~

Mix some Christmas green royal icing and stipple it on top of the cake to represent grass. Paint details onto the sheep and attach them to the cake with a little royal icing.

HATTON FLIGHT BARGE

25cm (10 in) square Sponge Cake, see page 6
strawberry jam (conserve), lemon curd or
Buttercream, see page 7
250ml (8 fl oz/1 cup) Apricot Glaze,
see page 8
1.25kg (1½ lb) sugarpaste
125g (4 oz) modelling paste
250 ml (8 fl oz/1 cup) Royal Icing, see page 8
liquorice black, berry blue, mint green,
Christmas red, melon yellow, tangerine and
dark brown paste food colouring
raspberry pink liquid food colouring

EQUIPMENT
30 cm (12 in) square cake board
no. 1 and 2 paintbrushes
plastic smoother
ball modelling tool
pieces of foam
1.25m (4 ft) of 1cm (½ in) wide blue ribbon

● Using the template on page 56, cut the basic shape of the barge, as shown in step 1. Cut a 10 x 7.5cm (4 x 3 in) oblong from the remaining sponge. Slice the cakes into two layers and sandwich with the filling of your choice if liked. Attach to the board with a little royal icing and assemble as shown.

● Hollow out the front and back of the barge down to approximately 5mm (¼ in) in depth, as illustrated in step 1. Remove the oblong from the barge, this will be covered separately. Coat the cakes with apricot glaze.

● Roll out 500g (1 lb) white sugarpaste and cover the barge. Colour 125g (4 oz) sugarpaste red, roll out and cover the oblong piece of cake, then attach to the barge with a little royal icing.

● Decorate the barge with different-coloured strips and shapes, as illustrated in step 3.

● Use modelling paste to make the bargeman, colouring and moulding it as shown in step 4.

● Use modelling paste to make a tiller rail, bucket, lifebelt and duck. Leave to dry, then paint on any details and attach the pieces to the barge with a little royal icing.

● Colour some royal icing blue and spread it on the board around the barge with a paddling motion to produce a rough watery effect. Add swirls of darker blue and white royal icing to give a little more depth.

● Paint any final details onto the barge, such as a name. Place a little blue royal icing in a greaseproof (parchment) piping bag without a piping tube (tip) and cut off the tip of the bag roughly to the size of a no. 3 piping tube (tip). Pipe some water ripples along the bottom edge of the barge. Trim the edge of the board with 1cm (½ in) wide blue ribbon.

EXPERT ADVICE
≈

When coating the board to resemble water, cover it completely with pale blue royal icing and paddle it firmly using a palette knife in a side-to-side movement as this will produce the required rough effect. Avoid stippling it by lifting and lowering the knife. Add swirls of a darker blue royal icing, again using the palette knife and the same flat movement. Finally, complete the water by adding a few white royal icing crests to the waves.

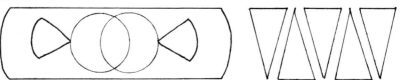

Pattern for barge sides

EXPERT ADVICE

≈

The barge can be decorated as simply or with as colourful a pattern as you please. Plant pots on barges usually have a black background with bright flowers. Always paint the flowers first, then outline them with black food colouring and fill in the background.

~ 1 ~

Cut the basic barge shape using the template shown left. Cut out the oblong cabin so that it is slightly narrower than the width of the barge and approximately 7.5cm (3 in) long. Place a 2.5cm (1 in) strip of sponge cake along the back end of the cabin. Using a sharp knife, hollow out both ends of the barge, down to 5mm (¼ in) in depth. Take care to keep the sides even and not to cut right through the cake.

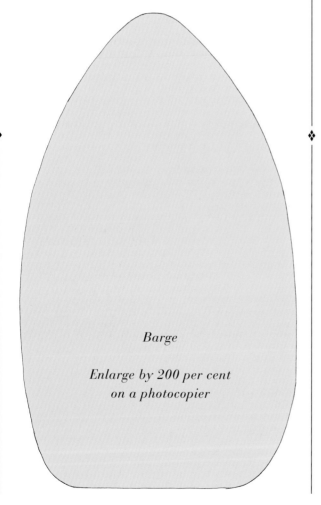

Barge

Enlarge by 200 per cent on a photocopier

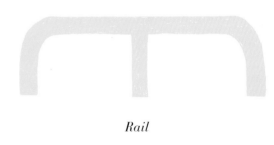

Rail

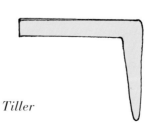

Tiller

Bucket

~ 2 ~

Remove the cabin, then cover the barge with white sugarpaste. Cover the cabin separately with red sugarpaste, then attach to the main barge with a little royal icing.

~ 3 ~

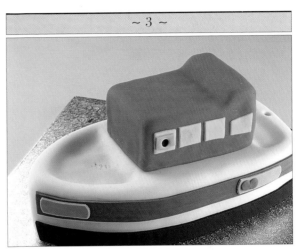

Colour several pieces of sugarpaste in bright colours. Roll out and cut strips or other shapes to decorate the sides of the barge. Follow the ideas used on the cake illustrated or vary them according to your requirements.

~ 4 ~

Colour a plum-sized piece of modelling paste chocolate brown. Model the bargeman's body, arms and legs, see page 13. Model a head and hands using flesh-coloured modelling paste. Model a flat cap in brown paste. Make a scarf and paint it when dry.

~ 5 ~

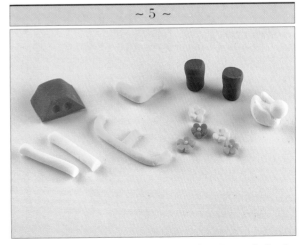

Model a bucket, rail, tiller, lifebelt and duck, following the templates on page 56 and the photograph of the cake as a guide. Model and paint flowers in pots if liked.

BOY RACERS

25cm (10 in) square Sponge Cake, see page 6
strawberry jam (conserve), lemon curd or
Buttercream, see page 7
250ml (8 fl oz/1 cup) Royal Icing, see page 8
125ml (4 fl oz/½ cup) Apricot Glaze,
see page 8
1kg (2 lb) sugarpaste
Christmas red, berry blue, melon yellow,
mint green, Christmas green and tangerine
paste food colourings
silver lustre powder
E Q U I P M E N T
25cm (10 in) square cake board
no. 1 paintbrush
no. 3 piping tube (tip)
ball modelling tool
1m (1 yd) of 1cm (½ in) wide red ribbon

Trim the cake, if necessary, so that it sits level, slice it into two layers and sandwich with the filling of your choice. Attach to the board with a little royal icing and coat with apricot glaze.

Colour 375g (12 oz) sugarpaste pale Christmas green. Roll out to 5mm (¼ in) thick and cover the cake.

Colour 125g (4 oz) sugarpaste grey. Roll the paste out thinly and cut two 30 x 6cm (12 x 2¼ in) strips. Lay these on top of the cake, curving them as shown, to form the race track, as illustrated in step 1.

Colour 60g (2 oz) sugarpaste dark grey. Roll the paste into 5mm (¼ in) thick sausage shapes and cut into 7.5cm (3 in) lengths. Stick three pieces together with a little water and curve to form crash barriers for the corners of the race track. Paint with silver arrows when dry.

Roll out a small piece of white sugarpaste thinly and cut out small oblongs and squares for advertising hoardings and to make a chequered flag. Leave to dry, then paint the details as illustrated in step 5.

Divide the remaining sugarpaste into five pieces and colour each piece differently: red, blue, yellow, green and orange. Use the coloured sugarpaste to model the racing cars, using the template on page 60. Assemble the cars, sticking the various pieces together with a little royal icing or water.

Colour a little royal icing green and spread it thinly around the edge of the race track. Stipple the icing to represent grass by dabbing it with a paintbrush held vertically.

Pipe a line of shells to neaten the bottom edge of the cake, using a no. 3 piping tube (tip) and green royal icing. Trim the edge of the board with the 1cm (½ in) wide red ribbon.

EXPERT ADVICE
≈

The race track is made from a strip of grey paste which is applied to the cake while soft. Being flexible, the paste is easily smoothed into a neat curve but it is important to remove the folds and creases as you work. If you are unused to handling sugarpaste, you may find it easier to cut a ring template to fit the top of the coated cake and use this to cut out the sugarpaste. The ring will be easier to smooth into place.

Car body

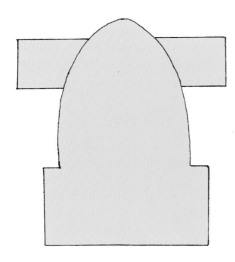

Back piece

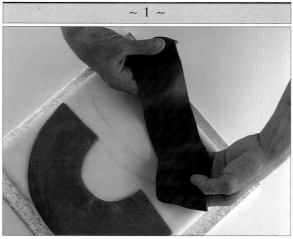

The track is applied in two halves, each a 30 x 6cm (12 x 2¼ in) strip of grey sugarpaste. Dampen the surface of the cake with a little water. Cut and apply the strips one at a time, curving them to meet in a circle. Ease out creases and smooth into place. Trim off excess.

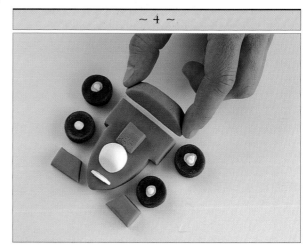

~ 4 ~

Using the template provided left, cut out five different-coloured car bodies. Cut two front pieces and one back piece for each car. Model five helmets and windscreens, and five graduated pieces which sit behind the driver. Stick the pieces together with icing or water.

~ 2 ~

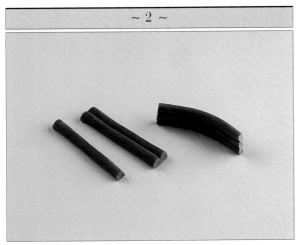

Make crash barriers by sticking three 7.5cm (3 in) sausages of grey sugarpaste together and curving them to hug the corners. Paint the silver arrows when the paste is dry.

~ 3 ~

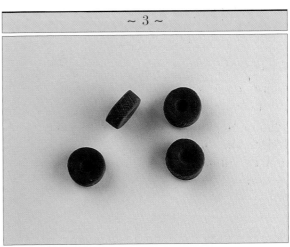

Make four wheels for each car and mark the criss-cross tread pattern with a knife.

~ 5 ~

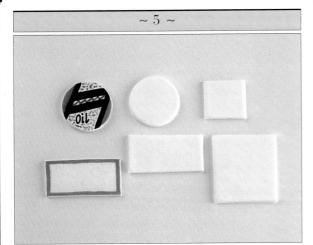

Cut out oblongs and squares of white sugarpaste and allow them to dry. Then paint the details for the advertising hoardings. It may be fun to devise advertisements to suit the recipient of the cake. Paint a chequered flag and pipe a message on it if you like.

Chequered flag

TEDDY BEARS' PICNIC

*T*his is a fun cake to make! Let your imagination run wild creating the birthday spread of your dreams, including goodies ranging from sausage rolls to chocolate fudge cake. Vary the colour of the tablecloth and the ribbon board trimming for boys and girls, if you like.

20cm (8 in) round Sponge Cake, see page 6
strawberry jam (conserve), lemon curd or
Buttercream, see page 7
125 ml (4 fl oz/½ cup) Apricot Glaze,
see page 8
375ml (12 fl oz/1 ½ cups) Royal Icing,
see page 8
1kg(2½ lb) sugarpaste
1 tsp red piping gel
1 glacé cherry, halved
5 chocolate-covered mini rolls
blueberry, dark brown, melon yellow,
liquorice black, Christmas red, mint green and
tangerine paste food colourings
raspberry pink and cream liquid
food colourings
EQUIPMENT
30cm (12 in) round cake board
plastic smoother
1.5cm (¾ in), 2cm (⅞ in) and 3cm (1¼ in)
diameter round cutters
ballpoint pen top
no. 2 paintbrush
ball modelling tool
no. 0, 1, 2 and 41 piping tubes (tips)
1.25m (4 ft) of 1cm (¼ in) wide pink ribbon

Trim the top of the cake level. Slice the cake into two layers and sandwich them together with the filling of your choice. Attach to the board, off-centre towards the back of the board, with a little royal icing. Coat with apricot glaze.

Colour 250g (½ lb) sugarpaste pale blue. Roll it out to 5mm (¼ in) thick and cut a strip deep enough and long enough to cover the side of the cake.

Colour 250g (½ lb) sugarpaste pink. Roll it out and cut a wavy-edged circle, at least 2.5cm (1 in) larger than the top of the cake. Lay the sugarpaste over the cake, as illustrated on page 64. Pinch and lift the edges of the paste with your fingers, to give a draped-cloth effect.

Colour 250g (½ lb) sugarpaste brown and model the bears, as shown on page 11.

Use the 3cm (1¼ in) round cutter to cut out 15 large plates. Use the 1.5cm (¾ in) cutter to cut out six small plates. Use the 2cm (⅞ in) cutter to cut out tiny saucers. Model a teapot, milk jug and sugar bowl, teacups and saucers as shown in the step-by-step photographs. Colour the remaining sugarpaste various colours and model the food as illustrated in the step-by-step photographs.

Colour some royal icing green and coat the board surrounding the cake. Stipple the icing to represent grass by dabbing it with a paintbrush held vertical to the surface. Attach the chocolate roll seats with a little royal icing. Fill a greaseproof (parchment) piping bag with any leftover green icing and pipe some grass around the bottom edge of the table and seats.

Trim the edge of the board with 1cm (½ in) wide pink ribbon, or a colour to match the cloth.

~ ❖ ~

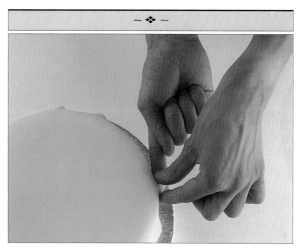

Allow the sugarpaste cloth to drape naturally when placed over the cake, then emphasize the effect by lifting and pinching the edges.

~ ❖ ~

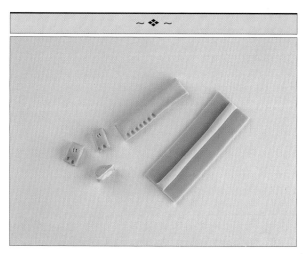

For sausage rolls, colour sugarpaste pale golden brown and roll out thinly. Cut it into 10 x 1cm (4 x ½ in) strips. Make long sausages of pink sugarpaste and attach one to the centre of each strip with a little water. Fold one side of the strip over the sausage and stick to the other side. Seal using the tail-end of a paintbrush. Cut into small rolls. Make slits in the rolls with the point of a knife.

~ ❖ ~

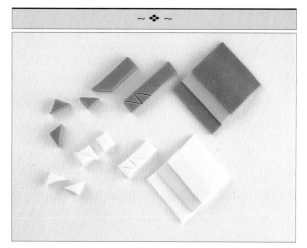

Make sandwiches by rolling out two colours of sugarpaste thinly. Sandwich the coloured paste between white or brown paste, brushing with a little water to stick them together. Cut into 1cm (½ in) strips, then into 1cm (½ in) squares. Cut in half diagonally. Stick to plates with water.

Cutter templates

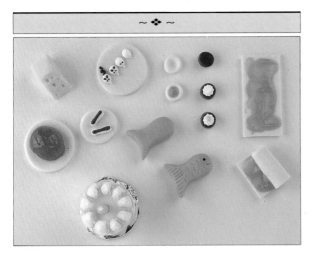

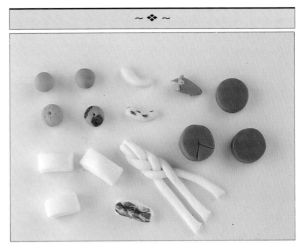

TOP LEFT: *Shape a small wedge of yellow sugarpaste to represent cheese, making holes in it with the tail-end of a paintbrush.*

Pipe mice with a no. 2 piping tube (tip) and a little white royal icing. Pipe a small shell for the body, adding black eyes, brown ears and tail, and a pink nose when dry, using a no. 0 piping tube (tip).

Use a sterilized ballpoint pen lid to cut bases for the tiny iced gems from rolled-out brown sugarpaste. Pipe on the top of each one with a no. 41 rosette piping tube (tip) and top with a spot of pink icing.

The jam tarts and Swiss (jelly) roll are made with pale golden sugarpaste; the tarts are the same size as the iced gems, indented with a ball modelling tool.

For the Swiss (jelly) roll, roll out a thin strip of sugarpaste to about 4 x 2cm(1½ x ¾ in). Spread with red piping gel and roll up. Moisten the top and sprinkle with caster (superfine) sugar. Cut a slice to lay beside the roll on the plate.

Model a fish out of orange sugarpaste, marking it by using the piping end of a no. 2 piping tube (tip).

Pipe eclairs with a no. 3 piping tube (tip). Pipe

a short straight line of white royal icing, leave to dry, then pipe a line of chocolate brown icing on the top of each one with a no. 2 piping tube (tip).

The jelly is half a glacé cherry with royal icing piped on top.

Make a mini cake from a small round of sugarpaste and pipe around the edge with a no. 41 rosette. Cut a cake candle short and place in the centre of the cake.

TOP RIGHT: *The fruit bowl adds a splash of colour. Model the fruit using coloured sugarpaste. Roll the oranges and strawberries on a nutmeg grater to give them texture.*

Sandwich two rounds of brown sugarpaste together with brown royal icing and dust with icing (confectioners') sugar to make the chocolate cake.

Plait three thin sausages of white sugarpaste to make the plaited loaf, then brush with brown food colouring.

MAKING CROCKERY: *Model the teapot, milk jug and sugar bowl out of pale holly green sugarpaste, painting on a pattern when dry.*

BEETLE MANIA

25cm (10 in) square Sponge Cake, see page 6
15cm (6 in) basin Sponge Cake, see page 6
strawberry jam (conserve), lemon curd or
Buttercream, see page 7
250ml (8 fl oz/1 cup) Apricot Glaze,
see page 8
1.25kg (2½ lb) sugarpaste
125g (4 oz) modelling paste
125ml (4 fl oz/1 cup) Royal Icing, see page 8
berry blue and liquorice black paste food
colourings
pink dusting powder (petal dust/blossom tint)
silver lustre powder

EQUIPMENT
35cm (14 in) round cake board
no. 2 piping tube (tip)
plastic smoother
no. 1 paintbrush
ball modelling tool
cocktail stick (toothpick)
1.5m (1⅔ yd) of 1cm (½ in) wide pink ribbon

● Turn the square cake upside down on a board and place the basin cake upside down on top. Carve the cakes to shape, as illustrated in step 1. The sides should be slightly sloping, so that the car appears to be narrower at the top than the bottom.

● Cut holes in the sides, near the front and rear, for the wheels. Slice the pieces of cake into layers and sandwich with the filling of your choice, if liked, then assemble and attach them to the board with a little royal icing. Coat with apricot glaze.

● Colour 1kg (2 lb) sugarpaste shocking pink, roll it out and cover the cake. Ease the paste gently over and into the curves, lifting out

and smoothing away pleats and folds as you work.

● Mark lines for the door, bonnet and boot immediately, with a sharp knife, as shown in step 2.

● Model the front and back wings of the car, as illustrated in step 3. Always start with two equal-sized balls of sugarpaste when modelling identical items, so that both end up the same size.

● Roll out the modelling paste thinly and cut out windows, windscreen, lights and number plate, as shown.

● Pipe royal icing windscreen wipers and window rims on waxed paper using the templates on page 68 and a no. 2 piping tube (tip). Paint when dry.

● Colour 250g (8 oz) sugarpaste black and model four tyres, front and rear bumpers.

● Paint the number plate when dry. Trim the edge of the board with 1cm (½ in) wide pink ribbon.

EXPERT ADVICE
≈

Always support unstable sugarpaste additions with pieces of foam sponge until they are thoroughly dried. For example, the wings of the car should be supported until the paste has dried.

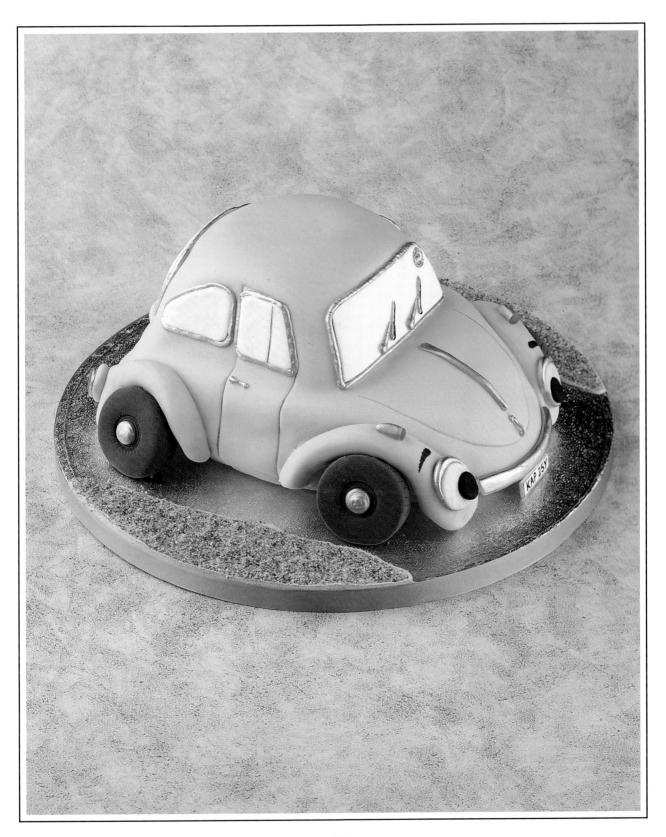

~ 1 ~

Cut a little off both sides of the cake so that it is wider towards the bottom. The bonnet is rounded and more elongated than the boot. Cut generous holes for the wheels as a little space is lost when the cake is covered with sugarpaste.

~ 2 ~

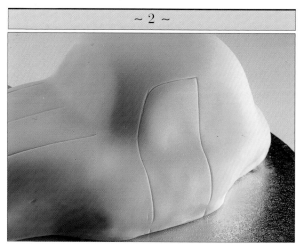

Using a sharp knife, mark out the doors, bonnet and boot. Be careful not to cut all the way through the sugarpaste.

HEADLIGHTS *Measure the width of the wings on your car, then cut out the lights to fit. Criss-cross the paste with a knife before attaching the lights to the car.*

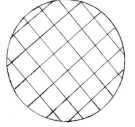

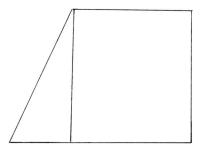

WINDOWS *Measure the side of your car before cutting the windows and check the exact size required. Then use the diagram as a guide to the shape.*

~ 3 ~

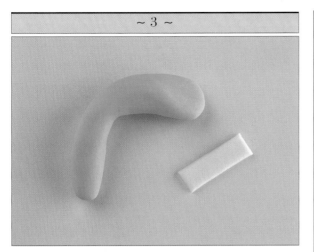

Using two pieces of sugarpaste the size of table tennis balls, model the front and back wings. Roll the sugarpaste into sausages, tapering them at one end. Lay in position, flattening the front end as you work. This is where the headlights will be positioned. Cut oblongs of thin white modelling paste for windows and windscreens, rounding off the corners. Roll a thin sausage of black sugarpaste for the bumper. Cut out headlights and mark lightly with a criss-cross pattern, also cut a number plate. Paint when dry and attach with a little royal icing.

~ 4 ~

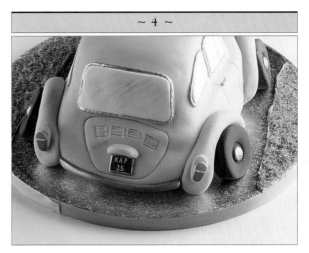

This is the back view of the car, showing the radiator grilles and lights. Cut out four wheels, marking them with a criss-cross pattern to represent the tread. Cut out the back lights for the car, attach and paint when dry. To finish, paint on any other details, such as VW sign on a small disk of modelling paste. Pipe royal icing door handles with a no. 2 piping tube (tip). Paint when dry.

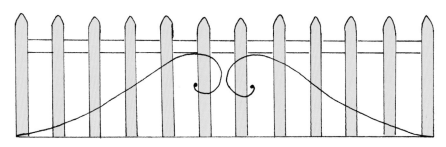

Auntie's Fireplace, see page 14
Fireguard

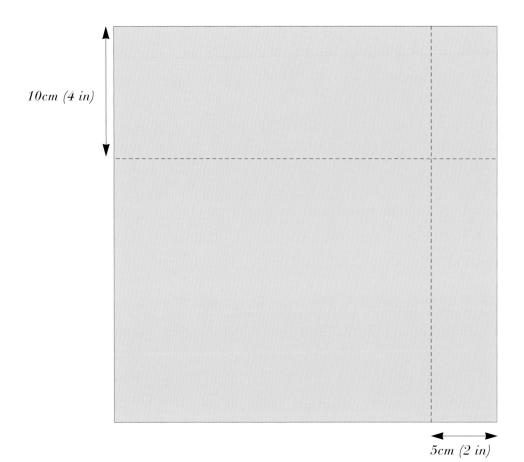

10cm (4 in)

5cm (2 in)

Cutting the cake

Two's Company, see page 22

Iceberg

Enlarge by 141 per cent on a photocopier

Walking Boots, see page 18

Heel

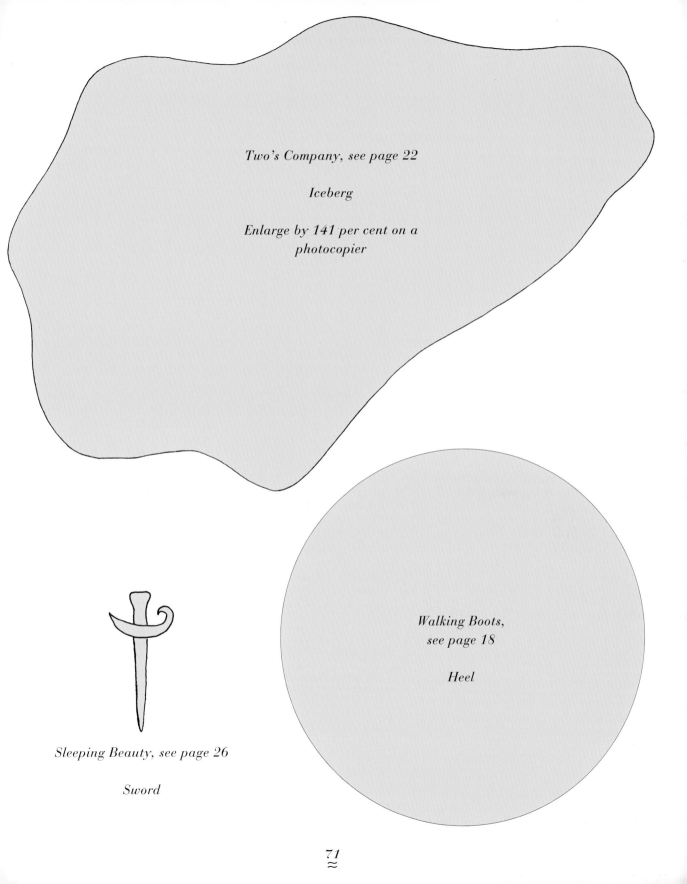

Sleeping Beauty, see page 26

Sword

INDEX

FOR FURTHER INFORMATION

Merehurst is the leading publisher of cake decorating books and has an excellent range of titles to suit cake decorators of all levels. Please send for a free catalogue, stating the title of this book:

United Kingdom
Marketing Department
Merehurst Ltd.
Ferry House
51 – 57 Lacy Road
London SW15 1PR
Tel: 0181 780 1177
Fax: 0181 780 1714

U.S.A./Canada
Foxwood International Ltd.
150 Nipissing Road # 6
Milton
OntarioL9T 5B2
Canada
Tel: 0101 905 875 4040
Fax: 0101 905 875 1668

Australia
Herron Book Distributors
91 Main Street
Kangaroo Point
Queensland 4169
Australia
Tel: 010 61 7 891 2866
Fax: 010 61 7 891 2909

Other Territories
For further information
contact:
International Sales
Department at United
Kingdom address.